Stand There
and Look
Pretty,
Darlin'

Stand There
and Look
Pretty,
Darlin'

Don't You Worry Your Pretty
Little Head 'bout Nothin'

MARY SUE RABE

Dedication

to

ALL WOMEN EVERYWHERE

And to Pat Pennington, My First Spiritual Teacher,
As well as to my loving Great Pyrenees,
SOPHIA and DAKOTA
My furry four-legged women

Contents

Acknowledgements

Special thanks to:

Beth Bruno   editing
Carla Rieger   coaching
Jean Huston   mentoring and foreward
The many friends who read my work and offered
suggestions: I appreciate your help.

Foreword

by

Jean Houston
Human Potential Scholar and Author of 26 Books

In these simply told but profoundly felt stories, Mary Sue Rabe offers us a vision of a society that is as potent as it is poignant. Growing up in a small town in Texas before the old ways of thinking and doing began to fail, we see this world through the eyes and heart of the wise child. Her deep feeling and love for the African Americans who worked in her home and on her family plantation gave her the strength to stand up for what she knew was both wrong and immoral.

Further, it was from these good people that she felt loved and nurtured as well as nourished. It was from them that she learned her most important lessons in values, in kindness, in perseverance in the face of all obstacles and what it was to love and be loved. Years later she sought them out all over the country, asking forgiveness for the ways that they had been treated.

Mary Sue lived through the ironies of a passing time when the worth of women was minimized by the culture in spite of their gifts and capacities. We see how all of her life she was one who crossed the great divide of "otherness". Naturally bright and filled with high dreams and complex ideas, she was told "Stand there and look pretty, darlin', don't you worry your pretty little head 'bout nothin'."

Then, there was the necessity to be involved in messy family money matters only to be told it was unbecoming to ask "bi'ness" related questions to the males in the family even if it is "your" bi'ness. After all they are looking after your interests.

What is unique in these stories of her life is the ways in which she faced the life of a woman in a time of dramatic transitions. We meet her confronting the old ways of being in expectation, business, racism, marriage, self-development. And we see how she has emerged out of the crucible of outmoded ways of being, inspiring and teaching other women and some very good men what this new time requires of us all.

She has become a beacon and beckoner for helping women embrace their power, challenging the way things are done, and ultimately building a new social order. Because of women's natural emphasis on process and growth, on making things grow, on inner life being as important as outer experience, women are more geared to team building and leading enterprises through natural growth stages. Governance, games, education, work, health, society itself can be held to a new standard--one that promotes and honors the fullness of who and what we can be rather than just collective rights and liberties.

Women like Mary Sue Rabe realize and are taking advantage of the fact that we are living in this time of the changing of the guard on every level, in which every given is quite literally up for grabs. It is the momentum behind the drama of the world, the breakdown and breakthrough of every old way of being, knowing, relating, governing, and believing. It shakes the foundations of all and everything. And sometimes, it even allows for another order of reality to come into time, including a dynamic partnership society between women and men. Throughout history there have been many cultural shifts, but what is looming before us now is a collective shift--faster and more complex than any the world has known. Other times thought they were it. They were wrong. This is it!

In this time of extraordinary transition, we can no longer afford to live as remedial members of the human race. A new set of values--holistic, syncretic, relationship and process-oriented, organic, spiritual--is rising within us and around us. These are women's values, women's genius, women's gifts. Though old forces and traditions and fears seek to restrain us, we know there is no going back. Our complex time requires a wiser use of our capacities, a richer music from the instrument we have been given. The world will thrive only if we can grow. The possible society will become a reality only if we learn to be the possible humans we are capable of being.

Many women are coming to see themselves as pilgrims and parents of this new emerging world and no old formulas and stopgap solutions will do. In the past, men in governments and the private sector have been partners in determining how the world works. It is time now to focus on the role that women, formerly largely excluded, should play in the development process. This is indispensable if we seek a future that is different from the past.

In all of this, Mary Sue Rabe has been a leader, a learner, a woman on the frontier of social change and human development. These stories of her early years are testament to the courage and resilience and the deep heartfulness with which she has worked to transform the world in which she was brought up.

This is happening all over the world. Women are indeed challenging the most sexist institutions from the medical establishments to business institutions, and at long last, their full creativity is beginning to be set free. In the course of my work in many countries in social artistry (human development in the light of social change) I am moved to celebration and gratitude for what women are doing to make a profound difference in these challenging times.

What is fascinating, and little commented upon, is how many women "of a certain age" like Mary Sue Rabe are taking the initiative across a wide spectrum of social change. Having seen their children grown or the equivalent thereof, they seem less fearful of personal consequences to taking the risks, creating and following through on needed communal projects, scolding, inspiring, teaching and making things happen! (Post menopausal zest is no mere metaphor.) The Dalai Lama recently said that it would be Western women who will save the world.

With all great respect to His Holiness, I find that although Western women surely have more advantages than most, it remains true that women everywhere are finding their power, trusting and developing their creative means, and profoundly making a difference in spite of what is often terrible backlash. In all of this Mary Sue has been fully present, leading the way to new ways of being and doing, and helping to create a world that works for all.

Introduction

I never thought of myself as a writer. It was never part of my "when I grow up" dreams or on my "bucket list" of things to do, as I do not like to write. But I do like storytelling, and I was encouraged many times by my mentor, Jean Houston, to tell my stories. She saw the writer in me and told me that I have lived the life I have in order to share it with others. These are stand-alone stories, not in sequence, that I have put together in this book as a memoir. Please forgive the repetitions.

When I began the nonprofit, Women Healing the World, I was thinking about all of the things that need healing, race relations being just one of the areas. How could I heal race relations? I did not have a good answer, still don't, but thought that one way would be for me to write a tribute to those who worked for my family with whom I had the most interactions while I was growing up. The unconditional love, support, compassion and certainly forgiveness I saw modeled by these employees had a deep impact on me. Their faith and resilience showed me the strength and courage to keep moving forward, no matter the lesson or the challenge.

Some of the stories I am telling here are about challenges in my life, situations that caused me to grow and change, to look at things differently, and to learn new perspectives from the person who was being my "teacher." I am not here to blame or "out" anyone, nor to be a victim, because I am not a victim, I am a student. I simply wish to recount my experiences and what I have learned along the path of my life. This book is about how I found my voice and learned forgiveness of others and myself along with unconditional love, things I practice every day.

My life has not been all "challenges," but I have learned the most through the trying times; therefore, these are the stories I've chosen to share. The fun times are certainly worth sharing, times of peace, bliss, and reward, but the lessons I've learned from overcoming challenges are what I have found most helpful. Maybe you will too.

Rules for Growing Up in the Fifties

I grew up in a small town in central Texas, the youngest of four children living in a "fish bowl," as ours was the biggest house in town. Appearances, manners, and what others thought were priorities to my parents.

Being raised in this conservative Southern environment, I received several unspoken messages:

1. "Stand there and look pretty, darlin'; don't you worry your pretty little head 'bout nothin'," implying that I would be taken care of and, therefore, did not need to know anything.

2. You go to college to get your MRS degree (a husband), and while you are there, it would be good to get a teaching certificate so you have something to "fall back on" *if* you should have to work. Teaching is the only acceptable profession if you have to have one; being a mother is the preferred job!

3. It is unbecoming to ask bi'ness-related questions to the males in the family even if it is your business. After all, the males are looking after your interests. Three sisters and one brother jointly owned property that we inherited, but only my brother made the important decisions about it. The sisters were told nothing. We were on a need-to-know basis—usually only if a signature was required.

I did pretty well following the number-one unspoken message, "lookin' good." I'm not sure how pretty I looked, but I did my best, always dressed up with makeup and coiffed hair in public, and I practiced my best manners. The only things I worried about were my weight, my clothes, and my boyfriend.

However, when I graduated from college without the MRS degree, I was unsure what I was supposed to do with myself. My group of friends was on the cutting-edge of Southern females entering the workforce, and we were not assuming the homemaker role. However, this did not happen by choice. The males our age were not stepping up with offers of marriage. I had never considered getting a job, but here I was having to go on interviews so that I could take care of myself. Where was that man who was supposed to take care of me? I felt tremendous pressure to get married, so I married the first appropriate guy I met after I started teaching.

I viewed him as a "knight in shining armor." He was good-looking, with gorgeous blue eyes, and he owned his own business that involved traveling abroad yearly. He was a "scratch" golfer who belonged to a country club, and he wanted to buy a house in an upscale neighborhood before we got married. All my requirements and those of my parents were checked off, and it was past time for me to be married. After all, I was twenty-five years old! So I did it—I married him.

It did not take long to realize that even though he looked good on paper, there were some big emotional issues that had to be dealt with. He had lost his temper a few times before we married and had frightened me, but I naïvely thought that if I could love him enough, these angry outbursts would dissolve. Boy, was I wrong! I ended up in therapy and felt like I was walking on eggshells, constantly waiting for the major crack. I was scared that I would say or do something that would set him off, but I never understood what that might be. Probably because it was "not about me." Yet I thought that everything was about me.

I did not realize or understand the pressures that the opposite sex experienced: the pressure they felt to marry, raise a family, and produce a lot of money to support that family. As I reflect on his perspective, I am reasonably certain that societal pressures and the negative voices in his head were not supportive and contributed to his unpredictable outbursts.

One Sunday morning I was dressing to go to church with one of my teacher friends. He was mowing the grass before leaving on one of his business trips abroad. I heard the front door open, the mower still running in the front yard, and suddenly the door to the bathroom where I was putting on makeup came crashing down. Lucky for me, I was at the opposite end of the room so the door did not hit me. He had fire in his eyes as he moved toward me. I turned my back to him and covered my face as he began to hit me. I was stunned. He hit me several times as I screamed and sobbed, asking him to stop. Finally, after his anger was spent, he calmed down.

The lawn mower hadn't stopped running on the front lawn, and the phone was ringing. I knew my friend was calling to see where I was, as I was late picking her up for church. I was in shock, and I think he was also. He became very apologetic and said he was angry from thinking of me seeing friends and having fun in his absence. We sat in silence. The mower finally ran out of gas, and the phone finally stopped ringing. Church was over by then. I was still very hurt when he left that evening for his trip, but I was relieved that he was gone so I could take a breath.

Another major outburst occurred after a wedding reception. I was by his side the entire time, as these were my friends and I wanted to make sure he felt included. I saw the bride's brother, who was also my friend, just as the newlyweds were about to leave in the limousine. It was great to see him and we hugged. Shortly thereafter, my husband and I got in our car to leave the country club and as we were driving away, my hubby accused me of going around to the pool area and having sex with the bride's brother. He was totally irrational. The man was like a brother to me and this incestuous idea was sickening. Moreover, the accusation was asinine, as I had been beside my hubby the entire time. His anger kept mounting. By the time we had gone a short distance he was so furious that he threw me out of the car, busting my lip in the process.

I stood on the curb in shock, with a busted lip and crying mascara rivulets. I must have been quite a sight in my long gown, standing there clutching an evening bag. All it contained was lipstick, a comb, and a handkerchief. That wasn't going to get me very far! Fortunately, a car with four young men pulled over. They asked if I needed help. I said yes and asked if they would give me a dime to make a phone call at the nearest pay phone. My plan was to call a childhood male friend who lived in the area and ask him to rescue me. The young men offered to take me to my friend's house instead of making the call. I was apprehensive about their offer, but when I found out they were students at my alma mater, I decided to trust them. They dropped me at my friend's house, doing a good deed, resulting in a good "pick-up story" about a woman stranded at a major intersection in Houston.

My husband and I **both** received counseling after this event, but we still divorced. I kept his behavior a secret except from my therapist, but I did a good job blaming him for our failed marriage. I allowed friends to choose sides—mine. I had been naïve to think I could "love him enough" to cure his issues, and that morphed into being naïve enough to think that it was all HIS fault. Naturally, my supporters agreed with me! He was to blame!

By the age of twenty-eight, I was divorced and alone again. Even though I had been trained to be taken care of, I just could not let that happen. While I was married, I had continued to pay all my own expenses. Something inside of me did not want to be obligated to another person, and I wanted control of my own money. Taking care of myself was not such a big deal, but living on a teacher's salary was! I could not support my previous lifestyle, and my biological clock was ticking. I wanted to have children—and soon! Where was that knight in shining armor?

It was during this time of being alone that I realized my conditioned life plan depended on another person. I could not achieve my goals unless I found another male to "take care of me." This realization made me angry, but I started looking. After all, the family did not like the fact that I had "divorced" (said in a whisper with shame), and that I was single again. My situation just did not "look right." I was sad that my "dream" life had become a nightmare, but I was willing to try again. I had just picked the wrong person.

A couple of months after my divorce, which took over a year to finalize, I found husband number two. He too looked good on paper. He was good-looking, had an Ivy League education, a good job, a sailboat, and a membership at a yacht club. Even though we had not previously met, we had many mutual friends, who, like the two of us, liked to party. We had fun for a couple of years until I got pregnant and alcohol was no longer my friend. We began to drift apart since we no longer had a common interest. I insisted on couples counseling where we worked on our relationship, which we tried to save by having children, taking a new job, relocating, and buying a big house, but nothing worked. Once again, on the outside everything looked great, but we were both miserable. I was doing what I was raised to do, but I was very unhappy. What on earth was wrong with me? All the promises of my upbringing were not leading to fulfillment for me.

When I quit looking at life through the green glass of Tanqueray gin, it became more real, not blurry. I wanted and needed to be present for my daughters so that I could be a good mother, but all I could obsessively think about was my husband and his drinking. I still wanted to have a good relationship with my husband. I missed the "good ole days" and all the fun we had, and I felt very alone as a parent. I envisioned welcoming him home with a cocktail and sharing our day, but he did not come home. By this time, he had decided it was more fun to drink with office friends than with me. You see, I had become an untreated Al-Anon, one of "those" people whose addiction has become the "user." I kept a tally of what I considered his bad behavior, counting his drinks, reminding him of commitments not kept, and constantly nagging and pointing out all of his shortcomings.

At night when I could not sleep for worrying, I read a book about what not to do if you are living with someone who drinks. I realized that even though I basically lived upstairs and he lived downstairs, I needed to leave. Maybe that would force him to quit drinking. We had a family that we needed to take care of, and he wasn't doing it right in my eyes. So, I began to make a plan. As soon as our baby was six weeks old and I could pick up a box after my C-section, I would move back to Houston and our former house, which had not sold, thank God. The bottom had fallen out of the housing market when we put it up for sale. I had spent all of my money remodeling our new big house, so I had to ask my parents for a loan in order to pay for the move. They were very upset and tried to talk me out of it. They even came to see my spouse the following Sunday and tried to get him to keep me from moving. He was ready for me to go; remember what I said about being a good Al-Anon? He was tired of my nagging.

So I moved, which fortunately led me to 12-step programs, the mysteries of life, and contentment. I was no longer searching for something or someone out there to "fill me up." I finally felt at home and knew that everything would be okay, no matter what!

Once again, I was pretty much on my own, but this time with the responsibility of two daughters, ages two years and six weeks. I had no job but got one at the insistence of my dad. (*Where is that man who is supposed to take care of me?*) I did not want to leave my daughters. I was supposed to be a stay-at-home mom, but they needed to eat and have a roof over their heads. I found a job, but most of my income went to childcare, and I really wanted to be at home. This was NOT how I imagined my life! Living on a teacher's salary was tough, and I ran up my credit cards trying to make ends meet. My widowed friend and I had many garage sales in order to feed our children. I was really struggling financially even though I received some funds from the girls' dad.

My life outwardly looked bleak, but I was happier than I had ever been. Yes, I did worry about money, but I realized that the worst thing that could happen was that I would end up on the street, pushing my daughters in a shopping cart with our two dogs tied to the handlebars. I would have all that I was responsible for right there and nothing else to be concerned about—no house to take care of; no clothes to wash; no mortgage payment, taxes, or bills. Relying on the 12 steps and the program people I met offered me much support, and I learned how to live life on life's terms. I forgave and accepted myself for mistakes I had made, including my second failed marriage. Even though I felt shame for a brief period over my behaviors, I always tried to "look for the good," so I decided that it was great that I had found not one but two men to marry me. Wasn't I lucky?

I had a friend at the time who would take me out to dinner, which was a real treat for me, as I could not afford to go out to eat. She was married to a wealthy man and had everything she wanted, yet she was not happy. She could not understand how I could be so happy when my life "looked so miserable." I shared with her that I was on a spiritual journey, taking complete responsibility for my actions and myself, learning to be grateful for what I **did** have and no longer looking for something on the outside to fulfill me.

I worked with a counselor regarding my probable, unwanted by me at the time, divorce. She gave me the Ho'oponopono prayer, an ancient Hawaiian Healing Ritual and said, "It's about forgiveness."

I said, "I don't want to forgive him. I cannot forgive him. He doesn't deserve it!"

She said, "Your lack of forgiveness is only hurting you. He does not know or care if you are mad, so who is holding the rope? You, if you don't forgive."

Eventually she convinced me to read this prayer every time I felt any angst, and I realized that as I read it, I became calm.

Strangely enough, my ex started going to the same counselor and her classes. We would end up in class together, along with his new fian-cée. One evening during a break, we were discussing our plan for him to pick up the girls for the weekend. A classmate overheard and looked at us quizzically. In reaction, I said, "Yes, we have mutual children." She was very surprised and said we did not exude the frenetic energy of divorced couples and even had a sense of peace between us. I had reached a place of acceptance, and it was not work—it was MAGIC! I attributed it all to repeatedly reading the Ho'oponopono prayer. It changed me for the better! I did not blame my second husband for our divorce. I realized my part in the demise of our marriage and did not want friends or family to choose sides, as we were both responsible. I even began to recognize my part in my first divorce…. Imagine that!

Even though we were divorced, we spent most holidays together with our daughters. When he was placed in hospice care, my daughters brought him to my townhouse where he made his transition. I felt blessed to be present in the sweetness and grief of this experience. We did not always get along, but I would have done anything for him, as I continue to do for our daughters.

As for my financial business challenges, I felt very alone in supporting myself and my daughters, and in retrospect I see that I created this condition because I didn't want to play the game of being the dependent female. I learned the hard way, in crises, to take care of myself and my finances. Since I had unwisely accumulated high credit card debt, I acquired a loan based on an interest payment due from the sale of some family property, not knowing that the property was being returned to us without any payments. This was when I learned I needed to ask questions and stay informed; otherwise, I would make more mistakes. This was also the time when I started speaking up, much to the chagrin of my brother. I now make informed decisions, despite some family members' objections, because I know it *is* "my business" and my responsibility.

It seems that I have always learned the hard way about how to take care of myself. How about you? Do you learn through grace? I learned that the only person I can depend on is ME. My biggest regret is that I did not know how to speak with the men in my life to express myself and be heard. I played the part of *femme fatale* as best I could, but being somewhat of a rebel it usually ended up being to my own detriment. I did not have a voice when I was in a relationship, and when I was not in a relationship, I did not know what to do. Now that I have found my voice, I speak up for myself. I am not abdicating my power to someone else. I am in control of my life and my finances. I find that now that I do speak up, my relationships with males are much clearer and more honest. There are no unspoken, hidden agendas. It has taken me a long time to learn this lesson, but I am glad that I have. Now I have a different perspective on women and how we behave or do not behave, and how we can contribute or not. I believe that if women become more involved in showing compassion for others and offering their support and opinions, whether solicited or not, the world can be a better place.

Women have been supporting men—invisibly, cautiously, and possibly manipulatively—for eons. Today, I suggest that every woman step up and be a part of every conversation. We need more heart in decision-making, not just heads. Now I celebrate the fact that I am a rebel. I have found my voice and I am dedicated to helping other women find theirs!

What Is White Guilt?

Can you be born with white guilt? I have pondered this question for years and still have no answer.

The first time I truly felt a twinge of empathy, compassion, and guilt, feeling like something was not right, was during a stay out at our house on the family farm in the Brazos River Bottom, known to us simply as The Bottom, during the summer when I was a little girl. I was sitting on the window seat at the top of the stairs of our two-story house, looking out the open window with a nice breeze in my face, when I noticed a little black girl about my age walking through the gate to our front yard. She was carrying a pail. She walked over to the water faucet in the front yard, turned it on, and filled her pail with water. She turned off the faucet and walked with her pail of water back out through the gate in the white fence that surrounded the yard. I wondered why she had done this as I watched her walk back to a small shack in a row of shanties that lined the road leading up to our house. I ran downstairs to ask my mother why this little girl would be in our yard filling up a pail with water. My mother's response was that the girl's mother had probably sent her over to get it. I was still confused, wondering why she was fetching water instead of playing like me, and the concept of having no running water in your own house was not on my radar as a four-year-old, but the knot in my stomach told me that something was not right. I felt sorry for the little girl who was having to "work" instead of play. Little did I know!

When I looked out that window again, I could see all the way down the road leading to our house to the highway. Lining the road to our house, on the right side looking toward the highway, were many little shanties. I did not realize until the late sixties that these houses did not have running water or electricity. There were many people who lived on The Place, which was a small community with a commissary where the residents would get their groceries on Saturday morning, and the cost would be deducted from their wages. My older sister remembers working in the commissary some Saturday mornings, bringing big sacks of flour, beans, or rice to the counter. She would fill the orders while an adult sat at the counter, added up the prices of the groceries, deducted the total, and then handed over the balance due the employee. Saturday mornings at the commissary were fun for me, as I did not have to work. I liked to chat with all the people standing in line to get their groceries and then go exploring around the sheds or to the slough to look for turtles or to throw rocks in the water to see the ripples.

One of my favorite foods from the commissary was summer sausage, sandwiched between two premium saltines. I loved the sausage with its big pieces of black pepper.

I had fun when we went out to stay at the house in The Bottom in the summer. My father had the house built around the time that he and my mother married. My mother had seen a home in *House and Garden* magazine that she loved, except for the staircase coming down in the front of the house. My dad had a fraternity brother at the University of Texas (UT) who received a degree in architecture, so the friend drew up the plans for the house as a wedding present, with the stairs coming down in the back of the house. This friend was B.W. Crain, who was one of the architects for the Astrodome in Houston.

My dad used to tell a funny story about the building of this house, as he wanted to have it finished by the time he and my mother were married. Unfortunately, the night the frame was put up, there was a terrible windstorm that tore down the frame, so the builder had to start over. Because of the storm, the house was not completed in time. When my parents returned from their honeymoon to New Orleans, they had to move in with my dad's parents, whose house was next door to the building site. My dad said that it took even longer to finish after they were married because my mother would go over and spend the day talking to the workmen. I can certainly understand, thinking about the house that my grandparents lived in and the lack of privacy!

It was fun to run around with no actual streets, just dirt roads. The farm was a very busy place in the summer, because early in the summer there would be truckloads of migrant workers who came in and chopped the cotton before moving on to another farm. I loved being there and sometimes got to help ring the bell to let everyone know when it was time to work, time for lunch, time to start back to chopping, and quittin' time. I liked to hear the sound of that heavy gong hitting the side of the bell. It was a deep, rich sound that vibrated through my small body.

Sometimes late in the afternoon or early evening we would go crawfishing down at the bridge over the bayou. I don't remember much about the crawfish, just that the event of going to the bayou with everyone was fun. I liked it when we were out in the country, as I was always included, while in town I was not always part of the group. When I say "everyone" I mean my siblings and all the "help" that was around. My parents certainly did not partake in crawfishing.

When my parents went out on Saturday nights they would leave us with Maude, our help out in The Bottom at that time. I remember thinking that Maude had terrible breath; she really smelled bad when she would hold me and rock me. I found out later that Maude was a drinker and that it was probably "beer breath" that I was smelling. My dad told me a story that one time when our family went to Fort Worth, probably for the Fat Stock Show, Maude, whom we took with us, disappeared for four days. I guess my parents figured her out because I never heard any mention of a missing person. She showed up the day we were to travel back home, and nothing was ever said about where she was or who she had been with. She just came back, no questions asked. I don't know what happened to Maude, but I did like her and thought she was fun, probably because she had a few beers under her belt while dealing with four children.

When we stayed out in The Bottom, I felt like a princess, and I assume that I was treated like one, too. At least I got lots of attention!

I remember one night in particular with a march of the masses to the commissary, which was just behind my grandparents' house by the bell tower. We went to the commissary for a treat, a Dreamsicle or a Snickers bar if we behaved ourselves. I wonder if any of the black adults in charge would have ever said that we had misbehaved. Anyway, one particular night when we were on our way to the commissary, there was a whole group of us, all four children and several black adult caretakers. I remember that I could not recall one young man's name, so to cover up that I could not remember, I called him Fruit Cocktail. You see, I loved fruit cocktail, and I thought that he was very fun and likeable. I believe that his real name was Willie B, the son of Virgie, who became the country cook, and James, the mason who built the brick walls around our driveway. Everyone thought his nickname was hysterical; it caused much laughter. I continued to call him Fruit Cocktail for many years.

Looking back on my childhood, I realize how much attention I received. I had all of these older people around me who treated me like a princess. Who knows if they even liked me? I realize now that I had a lot of power, unbeknownst to me at the time. I wonder how they felt, whether there was a concern about not pleasing me or one of my siblings? As I look back at the situation, I realize the balance of power, adults over children, was not happening here. It appears that I had all the power in this situation. Is that why they treated me so kindly? Now I am wondering and wish there was someone still alive to ask.

Life in the Brazos River Bottom began to change, with old ways making way for the new. Families who had worked for my family for generations encouraged their children to find other ways to make a living, and education was giving them more choices. There was also the invention of the cotton picker, a huge, expensive machine that could replace many people who picked cotton by hand. Machines and children choosing to move to the city left only a handful of residents still living on The Place. We were all evolving, progressing, but really? Yes, these people needed better living conditions, wages, and education, but wouldn't a week of this simpler life be refreshing for a moment? It was truly a community where everyone looked after one another.

Growing Up in the Segregated South

Told from the perspective of a little white girl. In the world of healing, what needs to be healed in me is my conflict about race, which began at a young age.

A few years ago, as I was applying for a passport, I closely examined my birth certificate and noticed my father's occupation was listed as "plantationer," which I'm not sure is even a word! I felt embarrassed and ashamed, as this word brought to mind flashes from *Gone with the Wind* of mean slave-owning white men. I was born in 1950. When I reflect about The Bottom—our family farm located in the Brazos River Bottom of Texas—I realize that it was operated like a plantation, but the workers who lived on The Place were not owned. There were many small houses for employees along the road leading up to the main house. There was also a commissary, where these employees got their groceries on Saturdays, so they never had to leave the farm. I shared my distress over my father's occupation with one of my daughters, who suggested that having that as a profession clarified that he was the owner and manager of a large farming business, whereas, if it had said "farmer," it would be referring to the one driving the tractor.

My parents purchased a large, two-story colonial house a couple of years before I was born in a small town in Texas; it was away from the farm, "in town." The house was built in 1901 and did not originally have indoor plumbing; therefore, there was an outhouse. My parents added bathrooms to the house but kept the outhouse, which was used by the help, who cooked, cleaned, cared for the children, and did the yardwork.

A loving black woman named Bea would come and spend weekends at our house when I was growing up. She and her twin sister were born out on what I heard our farm called, The Place, and they had no birth certificates. I also heard that she had pushed my dad around in a baby carriage when he was a baby.

Bea was a small person who always wore a scarf around her head and an apron over her dress. Her necklace held a dime and a fishing weight around her neck on a string. The dime she had received as change, and she wore it because it was unusual with a hole in it; the weight was to keep her nose from bleeding, or at least that's what she told me! She sometimes put a piece of straw or the end of a wooden matchstick behind her ear for dipping snuff. I still don't know exactly what snuff is or its purpose, for that matter. Bea's snuff came in a small tin silver cylinder with a lid that slipped off. Her earrings were broom straws placed in the holes in her ears to keep them open. When our family went on a trip in 1960, we bought her a souvenir of red ball stud earrings, which took the place of the straw. I don't know why it took us so long to get her some earrings! Her bed for the weekend was in the upstairs hall. It was a big hall, and to this day we call the bed she slept in "Bea's bed." There was a Navajo Indian print blanket on her bed regardless of the weather, which I still have. She brought her things in a dented, shiny black metal suitcase that she put at the foot of her bed. She had no privacy. My sister and I were recently wondering where she dressed.

My father loved to go out on Saturday nights. Therefore, on Saturday afternoons a family member would go pick Bea up, and she would stay with us until Sunday night after church, when either my father or one of my siblings would drive her home. She lived fairly close to us, in a small town called College Station, named for the actual station where the students that attended Texas A&M College would get on and off the train. We lived in the sister city of Bryan, where we had more paved streets than College Station at that time. The road to Bea's was mostly gravel, as were the streets in her neighborhood. She lived with her daughter and three grandchildren in a wood-framed house across the street from her church on the corner of Carolina and Holleman, with big green bushes around the perimeter of the yard with an opening in the center for a walkway.

Most Saturdays I rode with whoever was doing the pickup, as I was always excited to see Bea and wanted to greet her as soon as she got in the car. It was almost like having a friend over for a slumber party!

I loved it when Bea came to babysit on the weekends, as she was really good to me. She would tell me stories of Little Red Riding Hood or Brer Rabbit on Saturday night until I fell asleep. If I had a cold, she'd rub Bengay on what she called my "feets." She tucked me in and made me feel cozy and loved. She also recited the Beatitudes from the Sermon on the Mount, as she was a very religious person. She was like a kindhearted grandmother to me. I loved just being with her.

Bea made me greasy French fries and hot dogs for dinner, which I thought was great, especially the greasy fries. She peeled the potato, cut it into thick, long pieces, then placed the pieces in water until it was time to put them in the frying pan. After melting tons of Crisco in the pan over the heat from the burner, she put the potatoes on a paper towel to dry them some before putting them in the hot oil. I can still hear the popping noise as the wet potatoes hit the grease, and see the oil bubbling around them. Yummy, greasy fries with lots of ketchup!

My mother would put Bea to work as soon as she walked in the back door of our home. She ironed our cotton clothes or, sometimes, when we had pecans from the trees out in The Bottom, she shelled the pecans. We had a "built-in" ironing board that folded down out of a kitchen cabinet. Bea sprinkled the clothes, wadded them up in a ball, and placed them on the ironing board in order to have the clothes handy and ready when she finished one item. When she got ready to shell pecans, she would get some newspaper and spread it out on the kitchen table. She used a hammer to tap the shells; she had a nutcracker but rarely used it. The goal was to crack the shell and get the pecan piece out whole, but sometimes they ended up in pieces. She would have piles of pecans, whole ones and then the pieces. She let me snack on the pieces, but the whole ones were considered "prize" pecans.

Our family had a cabin at a place called Camp Creek that we owned with another family when I was young. Lots of families from the area spent spring and summer weekends at Camp Creek, waterskiing, swimming, or fishing. Our place was built on the side of a hill. When you walked in the front door, you were on the main floor with a big open room and a kitchen to the left. There was a bar with stools separating the kitchen from the big room. The bedrooms and baths, two on each side, were down hallways on either side of the kitchen. If you kept walking from the front door, there was a door leading out onto a large deck where you could look out at the lake and look down the hill to the boathouse and the pier that belonged to our property. Underneath the deck was a screened-in area, a place for Bea to sleep. I remember thinking it was creepy. I'm not even sure whether or not it had a light. I just know that is where she stayed when we went to Camp Creek and we always took her, probably so she could clean any fish that were caught. And I'm sure that the adults would go out, even if just over to someone else's place on the lake, so Bea would be there to look after the children. Since I was too young, or so they said, to waterski, I got to ride in the boat and sometimes I would get to fish, usually when Bea was fishing. I was young and impatient when it came to sitting still in order for fish to take the bait, but I do remember once I told Bea that I was not going in the house until I caught a fish.

Years later, I went to a high school graduation party that involved fishing and was so excited that I caught one. Bea was spending the weekend with us, so I took it home for her, as I was not really fond of eating fish at that time in my life. I remarked to her that this was the second fish I had ever caught; the first one was from our time on the pier at Camp Creek. She smiled and revealed to me then that I had never actually caught a fish at Camp Creek. She had put one on my line since I would not go in until I caught one, and she knew from my wiggling that catching a fish was not going to happen. I was sad to think that I had never caught a fish. Was I being humored, protected, or was she just realistic about this little girl who had her mind made up to catch a fish? I was always glad to have Bea with us at Camp Creek. Who would have kept me company if it weren't for Bea? Everyone else was waterskiing.

One time when Bea was staying with us, my brother came home with a rabbit that he shot while out hunting and he gave it to Bea. I was horrified that my brother had killed Brer or Peter Rabbit, but Bea took the rabbit outside and hung it on the clothesline, showing off her skills of "dressing" the rabbit. She skinned it and then gutted it to make it ready to eat as soon as she got home. I was so amazed at her skill with a knife that I forgot all about Brer and Peter. She thanked my brother and told him how much she enjoyed eating rabbit and how tasty it was. The thought of eating a rabbit was too much for me!

When at home, I went outside to play and sometimes got on my bike and rode all over the neighborhood for hours, not thinking about Bea and her wondering where on earth I was. She was supposed to be looking after me, and she couldn't find me! When I finally showed up, she would tell me that she was about to get a switch from one of the trees and come find me. I do not know if I ever believed that story, but I know it never happened! As an adult, I realize that I probably did cause her great worry when she couldn't find me. What if I had not returned?

Besides playing outdoors, I liked to play with my dolls. I was especially fond of Tiny Tears, a doll that looked somewhat like a real baby and wore doll diapers and baby clothes. Considering I played with the dolls so much, Bea decided to make a quilt for my baby dolls. Since the quilt was small, so were the strips of cloth that were used to make it. I still wonder how she did the sewing, such small stitches with her bent, knotty, arthritic fingers. I still have this doll quilt; maybe someday I will give it to a grandchild.

Bea fixed me fries, tucked me in, cracked pecans, dipped snuff, and ironed. I still miss her. I was a junior in college when I awoke one fall night and told my roommate that something bad had just happened. It was a very strange feeling. My dad called the next morning to say that Bea had passed away and it had happened right at the time that I had awakened. We ARE all connected! When I drive by the place where she lived with her daughter, I think of her and have fond memories of picking her up and bringing her home. I began to lose touch with her shortly after my mother died, as my dad employed a permanent housekeeper to live with us. Bea was no longer needed on weekends, or so my dad thought. But I still needed her; I needed the stability of Bea on Saturday nights. My dad and I did not communicate about what I might need, and he was unaware of how important and deeply connected I was to Bea. Not being with her on Saturdays was another loss for me. I was growing up and starting to hang out with friends on weekends so I would dismiss any thoughts of Bea and missing her. Our relationship faded, but not really. Even though I did not see her, my memory of her is still deep in my heart. She helped me to always feel loved; even if I had disappeared for hours riding my bike and caused her to worry, she always forgave me!

My Second Mother

Rodee was like a second mother to me, as she was our housekeeper and my closest companion for the first nine years of my life. She was my best friend. I think that I was closer to her than to my own mother when I was little.

Rodee started working for my family shortly before I was born. Somewhere I have a picture of me in a highchair with her feeding me. We spent many hours together, as my mother left her to take care of me while she did her various volunteer projects. Rodee was the one who put me down for afternoon naps when my mother was not home. She would sit with me until I fell asleep, and when I was a bit older she read me stories. In later years, it was Rodee who prepared my lunch as I came home from the neighborhood elementary school to eat, and then met me with a snack after school. All in all, Rodee nurtured and loved me like I was her own little girl.

I do not know what happened to Rodee's husband, but I do know that she was a single mom with five daughters! On occasion, her daughters would babysit my siblings and me (there were four of us) when our parents went out on a school night. They always came in twos, as none of them liked to be alone with just us in our big house. They were all very nice girls. The youngest was about a year behind me in age while the others were around the same ages as my older siblings. After being a single mom myself, I admire Rodee even more.

Besides taking care of me, Rodee cooked and cleaned, which was quite a job since we lived in a large two-story house with five bedrooms. I am not sure how she did it all, including making our beds every morning. She came every day after her girls went to school. She arrived around nine a.m. and left after the evening meal was prepared, around five p.m. It was a long day, working for us to then go home and take care of her own children!

She did the washing for the six of us. Everything was line-dried, as clothes dryers were not yet household appliances. The daily ritual was to hang the wash out to dry on a clothesline in the morning and reverse the task in the afternoon.

Of all the "jobs" she did at our house, my favorite was her cooking.

I loved Rodee's cooking, especially her fried chicken and apricot fried pies. I always wanted her to make fried chicken, which was my favorite food when I was growing up. After we reconnected many years later, she came to my home in Houston to visit with my sister and me. She agreed to show us how to make our favorite fried chicken. I had tried to imitate her chicken by using a gooey mixture of flour, milk, and egg. All Rodee used was flour! I could not believe how good it was with just flour. What really made her recipe special, though, was not the flour; it was the key ingredient—love. She knew how much we loved it, and she loved making it for us.

Sometimes my mother had Rodee cook Sunday lunch for us. Frankly, I cherished the Sundays when she worked, because then I didn't have to go to church and sit there and be still and quiet. I got to go home and "help" Rodee. Occasionally, I would get to make my special salad: a half a pear with a dollop of mayo and grated cheese on top. It was a recipe from my Betty Crocker's junior cookbook that I bought one day at Jarrott's, the pharmacy that had everything. Sunday lunch at home was a special day. We ate in the dining room, and used the good china, the crystal, and the silver. We were dressed in our good Sunday clothes, and we used our best manners.

The dining room table was a training ground for manners and

etiquette. I loved eating in the dining room! Under the dining room table was a buzzer that rang in the kitchen to alert whoever was in the kitchen that we needed something in the dining room. I adored it when Daddy would step on the button on the floor and the "buzz" would sound. Besides making us a fabulous meal, Rodee was there to serve, remove, and wash the dishes. I imagine that she missed going to her own church and being with her five daughters.

Rodee and I had many special moments. One day she was cleaning out the freezer and I was looking at all the different things sitting out on the counter. There was a juice can that had ice around the top. For some reason I decided that it would be something like a snow cone, so I put my mouth on it. When I pulled my mouth away, I ripped the skin off the inside of my mouth. To this very day, I remember the pain and how Rodee helped me handle it. She picked me up, hugged me, and rocked me until I quit crying, and told me I would be okay—and I was.

Another time, my friend Bill came over to play while our mothers went out and left Rodee in charge of the two of us. We were bored and looking for something to do, as this was back before television was popular. Somehow we came upon two big boxes of strike-anywhere stick matches, which we thought were really cool. As was customary, we wanted to be outside playing so we decided to take the matches and strike them while walking around the backyard. We would drop them and watch as they burned out.

My parents had just put in a new driveway, and the asphalt was still kind of soft. On the other side of the driveway, there was a compost pile. I don't know if it was Bill's match or mine, but one of us threw a match on the ground and the compost pile caught on fire. We ran to get Rodee.

She was surprised to hear our urgent summons that the backyard was on fire. She called the fire department, grabbed a broom, and ran outside. By the time the fire truck arrived, Rodee had beaten the fire out with her broom. She had also somehow reached our mothers, who pulled up shortly thereafter. The firemen, after making certain that everything was okay and the fire was out, got back in their truck to back out. Since the driveway was new and the asphalt was still soft, the very large and heavy firetruck had sunk into the asphalt. The firemen tried and tried to get it out, but the truck was stuck. They had to call a wrecker service for a tow.

Bill and I were already in trouble for playing with the matches, but this ratcheted it up several notches. "Look what you've done!" my mother cried. Rodee calmed everyone by not being too upset with us. She felt we were good kids just acting badly. In her own way, she stood up for us.

Rodee was my protector. She would save me from getting in trouble and would run interference when my brother picked on me. At an age when a small child is at the center of his or her own universe, Rodee was part of mine.

For the first six years of my life, my family went to Galveston in August, about the time of my birthday, and Rodee would go with us. We'd stay at the Jack Tar on the Seawall, *the* place to stay at that time in Galveston. Sometimes Rodee would watch me when I was in the pool; at night, when our parents went out, Rodee was the babysitter in charge. It's funny, because my best friend in college, Jane, went to Galveston to the Jack Tar with her family and took her caregiver, Carrie Brown. Galveston was very popular in the fifties, in part because of illegal backroom gambling, which I am certain my dad participated in.

The Jack Tar in Galveston was the place to go and to take your maid to be your babysitter at night. Rodee was away from her daughters then for a week, sometimes two weeks. I had a great time. I was glad she was there, but now that I look back on it, I think how difficult that must have been as a single mom. It never occurred to me to wonder who looked after her girls. I was glad she was with me! We spent every birthday together until I was seven.

Then in 1957, around the time of my birthday, my family took a vacation. We were in California on my birthday. I assume we had an itinerary, because I remember receiving a birthday card in the mail from Rodee. In the card was a flower handkerchief that I cherished and still have to this day.

As I got older, my mother would sometimes ask me what Rodee did when she, my mother, was not at home. I would give my mom an overview, not really thinking much about my reporting. I look back now and think that Rodee was probably really tired and my mom expected a lot from her on a daily basis. The questioning and reporting went on for a while and then Rodee was fired—fired for not doing her job, her job that I had been reporting on to my mom. I was devastated. I could not believe that I would not see Rodee any longer, and I felt that it was my fault that she got fired. If only I had told my mom something else. Rodee was my first major loss in life, and I lost her at the hands of my mother and then myself. I was so upset that I did not speak to my mother for at least a month. Rodee was like a second mother to me, and my real mother had dismissed her. No more Sunday lunches, no more fried chicken or apricot fried pies. No more Rodee. I was nine now and Rodee had been there since the beginning. I had a huge hole in my being, and I missed her terribly. I was really mad at my mom! I do not know if it bothered my siblings as much as it bothered me, but I had a hard time in her absence. I felt sad and lost. I had told my mother the truth, and now I was hurting. What if I had lied? Would Rodee have been able to continue?

Years later, when I was at Safeway, my new neighborhood grocery store after moving to a different area of Houston, I handed the checker my check, which had my name on it. She looked at it and then asked if I knew a Mary Porter from Bryan. I replied yes, that she was my mother. She introduced herself as Dorothy, one of Rodee's daughters, who had come to babysit when I was a little girl. It was so nice to see her! We continued to stay in touch for several years. She gave me Rodee's contact info and that is how we reconnected and she came to show us how to fry chicken.

Rodee worked really hard and lived her life in service to others. In many ways, I feel the exchange was not always fair or equal, as she had many jobs taking care of my family and a huge house. As an adult, I do not know how she made enough money or had any energy left for her own daughters. There were days when my mother would not get home in time to drive Rodee home and she had to walk, as there was no bus service. Her "neighborhood" was a distance away and a long walk, especially in the hot Texas summers or when a cold Blue Norther blustered into town. Rodee took it in stride.

Rodee loved me, and she told me so in a couple of letters that she wrote to me after our "chicken frying lesson" in Houston. I still have those letters, as they are very special to me. Rodee gave me unconditional love. She looked after me, took up for me, provided a steady hand, and corrected my behavior when needed. When she was dismissed, part of me left with her.

I do not believe that "white folks," parents in particular, ever realized the importance of the relationships with the hired help, the deep love and attachment to these caregivers, and the impact they had on the children they cared for. I was fortunate to have stable, trusted, honest, loving support from the "help" who surrounded me. For this I am truly grateful. My life is richer because of them.

Have you ever lost a dear relationship due to someone else's actions? How did you respond?

Breaking Down the Wall

January is a time of year that reminds me of another person who lived on The Place. James was a fifty-five-year-old African-American man who worked on my father's land. He was the handyman responsible for putting up and taking down our Christmas decorations for the front of the house. He would put "Merry Christmas," a wooden cutout painted red, on the bannister upstairs until just after Christmas, when he would return to put up "Happy New Year," which was cut out of the same material, but green.

There were other wooden decorations put out in the yard: a reindeer, a cowboy Santa with a campfire, and a standing Santa, along with a few other decorations that I cannot remember. But I do know that the yard was very "busy"—so busy that a friend once commented that our front yard looked like Woolworths, which was a five-and-dime store that carried lots of decorations. James also helped with putting up the tree, which was quite large since we had fourteen-foot ceilings and my mother thought we needed a really tall tree to fill up the space.

After New Year's, after I went back to school, James returned to town to take down all of the decorations. When he was decorating the bannister, he went out the door to the upstairs porch at the end of the hallway right by my bedroom.

One year for Christmas I received a ten-dollar bill from Santa in my stocking. I put the ten dollars on my dresser and left it there to decide how to spend it. When the holidays were over, I went back to school and when I returned home later that day, there was a five-dollar bill on my dresser.

I was bewildered and went to my mother and asked her if I had received a ten or a five; I was confused. She looked confused also for a few minutes and then smiled. As her face lit up with recognition, she said, "Yes, it was a ten. James was here today to take down the decorations and he was in your room. He must have spotted your ten-dollar bill sitting on the dresser. James never takes it all, so he took some and left some, and now you have a five. He left you change."

I was puzzled that my mother was so matter-of-fact about this incident and did not express anger or promise to speak with him and get my other five back. She had accepted that this was just the way he was. I realized that I was not angry either. If James needed five, I was glad to share with him, but I was grateful that he "made change," and I still had some money also. Five dollars in the mid-fifties would pay for lots of twenty-five-cent movies!

James was good with his hands, and his special talent was masonry. After my parents put in a new driveway, James came to town to build some brick walls around the new drive. It took him a couple of weeks to complete the task, preparing everything before he added the concrete. I was intrigued by his "level" and watching the bubble. The structure that he was creating had a solid set of bricks at the bottom and then the top had the bricks staggered so you could see through the top part, with each opening about half the size of each brick. These openings looked like a great place to put your feet and your hands, a perfect way to "climb" the brick wall. James finished the wall and after eyeing his work, cleaned everything up and packed his tools in his car to head back to The Bottom.

He was getting into his car when I decided to take my first "climb" to try out the new wall. I put my left foot in the lowest space with my fingers around the opening near the top and began to pull myself up. James jumped out of his car and was saying, "Noooooo," as I pulled myself up onto the wall. Suddenly it began to crumble and fall over. The cement was still wet and could not stay together with my little hands and feet pushing and pulling on them. The bricks, still with cement on them, were at my feet. I never even fell over but just jumped off in time to avoid injury.

I was embarrassed that I had caused the wall to fall and ruin James's work. James opened his car trunk, grabbed his tools, and began cleaning the cement off the bricks before it hardened more, as he knew that he would need to start over the next day. He did not react to me. He just went to work. If it had been one of my relatives, I would have been in big trouble. But James did not say a word; he just did his job. I cannot imagine being in his place when this thoughtless little white girl had just ruined his entire day's work. He was a good sport, but did he have a choice?

James was a nice-looking man. He'd been married to Virgie, a woman who also worked for my dad. She was a great cook, making everything very tasty. When I think back and remember the yummy food she made, it's a wonder that no one died of clogged-up arteries. She could make vegetables into carbs, as her squash casserole had lots of ground crackers, onions and cheese. You could barely find the squash, which was the way my dad liked it! She was great at disguising those healthy veggies. Okra was fried crispy and the fresh peas in the summertime were delicious, with pork fat cooked in. And those real chunky mashed potatoes with thick cream gravy did not need a disguise! Rolls were homemade fresh daily and the desserts were fresh every other day, usually a pie with lots of meringue, which was awesome. I did not partake of breakfast, but I am certain that it was terrific also, with eggs, bacon, sausage, and biscuits with lots of gravy or syrup. It's no wonder my dad had a triple bypass later in life!

Besides cooking, Virgie also washed and ironed the family sheets, as they were all cotton and quite wrinkly in those days. If breakfast, lunch, and ironing were not enough to keep her busy, she also looked after my dad's secretary's toddler for several years until she started school.

I remember a time when the stove at the house out in The Bottom, where all of the delicious food was prepared, would not stay closed, so Virgie propped it closed with a broom. My stepmother stated that we could not let Virgie come to town as she might see our kitchen and want a new stove. I was confused by this because I think that my family could easily afford a new stove. After all, cooking was her main job and she did it so well; she needed the right equipment!

I am not sure how long James and Virgie were married, and I do not know why they split up, but I do know that they had a son, Willie B, the one I renamed Fruit Cocktail.

Years later, when I was in high school, James came to our house to do some carpentry and while he was there he spotted our very attractive "city" maid, Mazell, who was much younger than he was. I guess he was a schmoozer because before I knew it, Mazell was dating him. This was in the late sixties, during the time of soul music, and there was a song that was popular by Candi Station called "I'd Rather Be an Old Man's Sweetheart Than a Young Man's Fool." I loved to tease Mazell, so I would put the vinyl record on my stereo record player with the sound turned up really loud and sing the lyrics to her until she blushed. I would then turn the music off and we would laugh and talk about guys and their silly behavior. She was a very wise woman, or at least she appeared to be to a seventeen-year-old! Mazell had a nice build, light skin with a pretty complexion, straightened black hair and a tooth with a gold cap around it with a star cut out of the middle, which always intrigued me. This style of cap was a popular way to decorate yourself back in the sixties; maybe today she would have a tattoo or a pierced nose. Mazell was a city girl; she never lived out on The Place, but she had James wrapped around her little finger!

When I think about James, I feel warmth in my heart. I still regret making his brick wall tumble, but he was always such a kind, patient man with a smile on his face. Thoughts of Virgie make my mouth water, while thoughts of Mazell make me giggle! All these people who helped make our life easier also helped shape my life in wonderful ways. I will always be grateful for them.

Postscript

A year or so ago, a wonderful young couple bought the house I grew up in. It had fallen into disrepair, as the previous owner had not taken care of it. It had lots of rotten wood, the banister from the porch on the second floor had fallen, and some windows were missing glass. This beautiful home looked like a haunted house! The house needed lots of work, but thankfully this couple was up to the task. They have been so kind to me and the rest of my family, asking lots of questions about what went on while our family lived there, what it was like to grow up living in such a grand home, and what the residents were like. The wife and I became fast friends, as there was an instant connection. We share a meal often and have wonderful conversations, like we have known each other forever!

As part of their renovation, they decided to put a fence around the property. It would be wrought iron with brick columns. In order to carry out this new design, some of the remaining fence, built by James, which had been standing since the mid-fifties, needed to be moved. When one of the columns was about to be picked up, it fell completely apart, to reveal a bottle in the center of the brick column—a bottle of tequila! The bottle still had a swallow of liquid in the bottom, after all these many years! No wonder James was so nice to me. He had something to "take the edge off." I'm guessing that he had his bottle and was about to get caught when he had to place it inside the column and keep working, only to hide his liquor from not only my mother or one of us children, but also from himself! I wonder if it was left in the center of the column because he forgot he put it there or if there was a quick need to stash his booze. I wish I could go back in time and observe what happened that day!

Have you ever wished that you could to go back in time to "spy" on a situation? What would you do if your truth was different from what really happened?

Forgiveness Freed Me from Decades of Burden

Did you ever make an innocent mistake as a child that grew to haunt you as an adult? That's what happened to me. I grew up in a plantation-like environment. There were many African-American people who worked for my family, and they were not treated equally in my eyes. There were many people who lived out on The Place, as the farm was called. Even though I never lived on The Place, lots of the people who lived and worked there came into town and worked for my family. One of these people was a lady named Bea, who supposedly pushed my dad around in his baby carriage. She was born out on The Place. When I was a little girl, she would come on the weekends and take care of me and my siblings because my parents went out every Saturday night. We had a bed in a long, wide hallway for Bea, and to this day we call it Bea's bed.

Bea had three grandchildren: Johnnie, Alton and Alma Jean. As I recall, Johnnie left Texas after graduating from high school and moved to California. When I was about five years old, one Saturday night Johnnie was in town and came over to visit his grandmother at our house. We lived in the largest house in town. It was built in 1901 and had an outhouse out back. The people who were employed by my family were expected to use that outhouse. Well, on this particular evening while Johnnie was visiting his grandmother, he used the restroom in the house. My job at that particular time in my life was chief tattler. I had three older siblings, and it was my job to keep my parents informed of all the things my siblings were doing wrong, or that they shouldn't be doing, at least in my eyes.

Johnnie was no exception. When he used the restroom in our house, I immediately ran upstairs and told my parents, because I knew that what he had done was not right. Now, being the chief tattler, that was all I thought about: tattling. I never really thought about the consequences of my tattling. To my surprise, my father was very upset, and he immediately went downstairs and told Johnnie that he knew better and he needed to leave. Johnnie very graciously obeyed my father and left, cutting short his visit with his beloved grandmother. When I saw what had happened, I felt ashamed of myself, as my mother often told me I should be for other unrelated acts. My parents finished getting ready and left the house for the country club and dinner. Bea and I were left alone at home. I don't remember talking to Bea about how badly I felt, but I remember thinking how Johnnie had come all this way to visit his grandmother and had been told to leave. Not only was he being punished, but Bea was being punished because of my behavior. I was guilty of tattling and causing this disappointment.

This incident was something that would occasionally surface briefly in my awareness, only to be pushed back in the recesses of my memories. I feel like I was carrying it as a subconscious burden for decades. A few years back, I started an organization called Women Healing the World, and one of our missions is to heal race relations. I realized that I had to start with me. And not knowing what else to do at the time, I began by writing stories, tributes to the people who helped raise me, because I really do appreciate all they did for me. They were part of molding me into who I am today. I hope that they enjoyed taking care of me. I appreciate that they were always kind to me. Then, I started to write a story about Bea, and I remembered this incident with Johnnie. All the guilt and shame surfaced again.

I decided that I would try to find Johnnie and apologize. I managed to finally get a phone number for his sister, Alma Jean. It then took me another couple of weeks to gather the courage to call her. Finally, when I did call, I was really upset, because I had finally gotten up my nerve, and she was not taking calls at the time. I left a message, unsure if she would ever call me back, but she did a day or so later. When I saw her name on my phone, I was so excited. I answered, and we began catching up with each other.

She had moved to California but was now back in Texas living in Pearland. I finally asked, "Could you give me Johnnie's phone number? I want to call him and apologize for an incident that happened when I was a little girl."

She said something like, "Oh, that. Yes. Okay, here's his number."

"So you know what I'm talking about?" I asked.

"Oh, yes," she said, which made me feel even worse, and concerned about his possible reaction.

She and I finished our conversation and hung up. I was excited and scared at the same time.

Having Johnnie's phone number filled me with all sorts of emotions: excitement, anxiety, and fear. I was thinking, *What if he is angry and yells at me? Maybe I should leave this alone and not stir up any trouble.*

Finally, I decided I would call him. This was something I needed to do for me, if not for Johnnie, if not for the African-American community around here and my ancestors. I needed to do it to let go of some of my guilt and shame. I dialed his number, and he answered.

We chatted a few minutes about the weather, and then I asked him if he remembered the incident when I was a little girl when I tattled on him for using the restroom inside our house. He said yes, he remembered. I told him how sorry I was about that, and how sorry I was that my father made him leave, and how I had felt bad about it for years.

He could not have been kinder. He said, "That was the way it was at that time." And he understood why it had happened.

I said, "I don't understand how your race could repeatedly put up with our behavior that way."

He said again, "It's water under the bridge. It's just the way it was at that time."

"How can you always be so kind, and how can your family always be so kind?"

He said, "My mother was very religious and she would always remind me that someday we would all know better. Well, hopefully we know better now and are treating people better."

"I hope you are right, and, again, I want to say how sorry I am for being so inconsiderate of your feelings. And sorry that my family treated you that way, too."

Johnnie accepted my apology, and my apology for my dad and my family.

I had always been concerned about how my family treated people.

Johnnie said that my dad was good to them. He reminded me that Bea's husband, his grandfather, ran the commissary. This was the store where all the people on the farm would get their groceries on Saturday mornings. I didn't remember that. What was amazing about him telling me that was that I'd had a strong flashback of that commissary as a child.

Several months earlier, I was at a personal growth salon with Jean Houston. She asked us to go back to a time in our life that was still keeping us stuck in the present. I had a vision of a little girl standing in the doorway of the commissary between my grandfather and an African-American man. I was standing there picking up on all the positive and negative feelings that these two men felt toward one another, all the things that were going on in the energy field, and how confusing it was to me. I wonder now if the African-American man in my vision was indeed Johnnie's grandfather, Will Richardson. Hopefully someday I can find a picture of him and see if that's the vision I had.

Johnnie and I talked about going out to the farm sometime when he was in town, and I asked if he would share stories with me from growing up. He did repeat that my dad was good to his family, and that his grandfather would sometimes have too much to drink and end up in jail.

I said, "Yes! I remember the phone calls on Sunday morning from the jail, and my father would always say, 'I'll be there after church and lunch to bail him out.'"

The calls weren't always just about Johnnie's grandfather, though. This happened with any number of people who worked for my dad. Johnnie and I laughed. He remembered being with his grandfather, who yelled at my dad, "Hey, Mista Hollan, what you white folks doin' today?"

Then my dad would reply, "Now, how much money is it you want to borrow, Will?"

What a conversation. Anyway, Johnnie and I finally hung up the phone, but not before I asked him to please get in touch with me when he came to town.

I felt so relieved. It wasn't just the normal kind of relief, either. I noticed my whole body relax at a deeper level. I noticed what a deep breath I could now take. I felt this huge openness in my chest. It felt like all my cells had been watered, and that they were all juicy, and dancing, and electrified. I had a difficult time going to sleep that night; my body felt excited, like tomorrow would be Christmas!

I felt as if a huge burden had been taken off of me. It didn't happen all at once, but I noticed a new energy, a new release, and such happiness at having such a great conversation, such an open conversation. I do hope that this is the beginning of healing many race relationships, not just those that impacted me, but that have impacted many other people. I truly felt the body/mind connection. I had stored guilt and shame in my body for sixty-two years. It's truly amazing what joy I felt, and how glad I was that I reached out and called Johnnie to apologize.

As I was writing this, I began to cry, wondering how they felt about me, as they all had and still have such a special place in my heart. I know Rodee, our housekeeper for the first nine years of my life, loved me because she wrote to me and told me so. I still have those letters. I am pretty certain that Bea loved me, too, as I feel certain she came to tell me goodbye the night she died. I cry now because I never told them how much they all meant to me. I hope that I was loving to them, as much as I was allowed to express, and I think that I was entertaining, as I was a funny kid. I liked to make people laugh and smile. They brought love and joy to my life; I hope I did the same for them.

Is there someone you need to forgive? Is there someone who needs to forgive you?

The Slingshot Gift

Ury was a short, small-framed African-American man who lived out in The Bottom. He usually wore a cream-colored felt hat over his curly hair. He had a huge knot on the left side of his forehead; no one ever knew what caused it or if it was a health risk. I am uncertain what he did besides being our yardman in town, but I am certain that he did more than just our yard!

Ury always rode to town with Walter, our other yardman, who drove the big flatbed truck, sometimes with the sides on, but most often just the flatbed. Walter was a tall, thin man who wore khaki pants and a long-sleeved shirt with the same sort of felt hat as Ury. Walter had long, skinny legs, so long that my dad named his birthday present canary "Walter" because of the canary's long, skinny legs. Walter was a quiet man who spoke few words but was always watching me. He had a wife and many children, while I believe that Ury was single with no children, at least none I was aware of. I think that Walter and Ury were friends, but I am not absolutely certain. I do know that Walter was the "boss" of the two of them; he had more responsibility and instructed Ury as to what to do.

I am certain they were very hot in the Texas heat, as perspiration would sometimes soak their shirts and roll down their faces. Even though they were hot, they were served lunch out on the back porch. I remember asking why they could not come in the house to eat and was told that they needed to eat outside because they were dirty from doing yardwork.

As I remember it, Walter would push the lawnmower (this was long before riding mowers) while Ury followed behind with a rake and a wheelbarrow to take the clippings to the compost pile behind the garage. I followed Ury, and then came my dog Snowball following me. We had quite the parade. I am not sure why I thought following them was such a special event, but I did. There were not many neighborhood kids to play with so I tried to play with Walter and Ury.

Ury was more apt to "play" or at least talk with me. He was always talking to me about my dogs, Snowball and Pepper. He worried about Pepper chasing cars, and rightly so, as Pepper lost an eye to a car tire, and then later, his life. No one told me until many years later that Pepper got hit by a car. They just told me that he had run away. I was protected from the sadness of losing my dog. Not only was I a gullible girl but also this was part of the "don't you worry your pretty little head 'bout nothin'" message that I was being raised to believe!

I am not sure if Ury liked to work, or if he was more interested in smoking and visiting with me. I think I caught some glares between Walter and Ury, as Walter would always keep working while Ury might take a seat on the steps and have a cigarette.

Ury made slingshots for my brother and me. He had some wood that he carved a handle out of for the part you would hold in your hand, and then a V-shape out of the middle of the wood. He drilled a hole in the top of the two V-pieces, put part of a rubber band through each hole, and then tied each end of the rubber band to the tongue of his shoe, which he cut out in order to have something to hold the pebble with to shoot it. I remember when he gave me my slingshot and explained how it worked, saying that the fabric piece was the tongue from his shoe, I felt like he had made a big sacrifice for me by cutting the tongue out of his shoe, and I still do. He took real pride in the slingshots, something he had made for us! He was always so kind and

I really appreciate the fact that he spent time with me. Maybe he didn't like working, but I'm glad that he chose to chat with me. It was always an enjoyable day for me when they were at our house.

Walter was the quieter of the two, or maybe I just engaged with Ury more because he rolled his own cigarettes, which I found fascinating. These days I feel guilty about Ury and his cigarettes, as I insisted he teach me how to do it and allow me to roll his cigarettes for him. I wonder how much that cost him? And what a position I put him in as the boss's daughter. How on earth could he have told me "no", as I am sure he would have liked to!

I assume that he bought his tobacco at the commissary there on The Place in The Bottom. The tobacco came in a small white cloth bag with a golden yellow drawstring. On the front was a blue paper pocket holder where the papers to roll the tobacco were kept. I am not certain why Ury rolled his own cigarettes, but when he took his bag of tobacco out of his shirt pocket, I was mesmerized. He would pull one of the small white papers from the holder and begin to curl up the sides of the paper toward one another; then he would carefully tap tobacco in the middle of the half-bent paper. When he had enough tobacco on the paper, he would put the golden yellow string in his mouth and pull to close the tobacco bag while keeping the paper between his arthritic fingers. He would then roll one side in and then the other until the sides met and the roll was complete. When he got the sides of the paper together, he would lick the seam to hold the cigarette closed and then twist the ends. Voila! A cigarette ready to smoke!

Even though Ury was a roll-as-you-go kind of smoker, I convinced him on several occasions to let me roll some cigarettes for him for future use. I was not very good at it, and I ruined several. It was much more difficult than it looked when Ury rolled them. Often I would mess up, not having the coordination to hold the paper and gently tap the tobacco onto it. I am certain that my "ready-made" cigarettes were more expensive than the ones he rolled himself, as I ruined some of the papers and spilled some of the tobacco.

I lost track of Ury as I grew up, although I know that he continued to live and work in The Bottom for years. Finally, one day when I asked about him, I was told that he had passed. I'm not sure when or how, but I still remember his attention and kindness.

From "Servant" to Friend

When I was growing up, my grandmother, who lived in Caldwell, Texas, was very proper. Her husband, my grandfather, was a self-made man who began earning a living at an early age. He became a "trader" and traded his way into acquiring some farmland, which he grew into thousands of acres of cotton. With such a large farm, he had many employees, most of whom lived on The Place, as the farm in Burleson County in Central Texas was called by the people who lived there.

Lillian was my grandmother's maid. She worked at the house in Caldwell and, I assume, at the house out in The Bottom, as the Brazos River Bottom was called. The river bottom was a large agricultural area in Burleson County along the Brazos River. I am sure that my grandmother had other maids before Lillian, but I remember Lillian the best because she also helped my family through the years, especially on holidays.

In 1956, when I was six years old, my parents went on a fishing trip with a cousin named Bob Oldham, who had grown up just down the street from my dad in Caldwell. Bob and his wife, Louise, had a daughter a year younger than I, Nancy, so when our parents went on the fishing trip, they sent the two of us to Caldwell to be with our grandmothers, who lived a block apart. We had the best time, running back and forth between the two houses, playing outside in the summer Texas heat, and getting hot, sweaty, dirty, and happy! Miss Annie, as Nancy's grandmother was called, played the piano by ear, which amazed me.

Miss Annie was very entertaining and could play any song we could name! She also taught us how to play a card game with her called Flinch. It was quite fun, competitive, and helped motivate us to stay inside to cool down in the heat of the day. Arnie, my grandmother, was all about cleanliness, so I was constantly having to change clothes. Nancy and I would walk about a block to the town square to get an ice cream cone. It was so hot that the ice cream immediately began to drip down the front of my shirt; I could not lick it fast enough. In a short time I had sticky drips of chocolate ice cream covering my shirt. As soon as I got back to Arnie's and she saw me, it was time to change into clean clothes. It's a good thing my mom sent lots of clothes, because I was wearing about six different outfits a day. Arnie did not have a washing machine in 1956; it was Lillian who had a big pot out in the backyard where she washed the clothes. Arnie's dryer was the clothesline where all clothes were hung to dry, and although it was humid, it did not take too long since it was so hot! I had always known Lillian, but we became closer on this visit as I was always passing my clothes to her to wash, and she would insist that I get in the bathtub for a quick bath before putting on the clean clothes since I was hot and sweaty. Lillian made sure I had lots of talcum powder all over my body to keep me dry and not so stinky.

After our time together during my stay at my grandmother's that summer, I would only see Lillian on holidays or when our family had a special event. She would be there to cook, serve, and clean up.

The Civil Rights Act had been signed in 1964, but in 1968, when I was a senior in high school, you might not have known that in this part of Texas. On some school days I ate lunch at the local drugstore, which had a great grill. My grandmother, who was living in a retirement community in Bryan at that time, while still keeping her home and most of her possessions in Caldwell, sometimes joined me. Lillian, who continued to work for my grandmother, went to the retirement community every day to look after Arnie. A few days a week, she drove Arnie to Caldwell to check on her house and to see friends still living there. Some days, Arnie had Lillian drive her to the pharmacy for lunch. Lillian could have a burger, but she had to go to the car to eat it, no matter the temperature. By the new laws, she was allowed to eat inside, but my grandmother still had her rules and Lillian knew what they were and ate in the car. Lillian "knew her place," but she was devoted to my grandmother, Miss Alma, who was called Arnie by the grandchildren. Lillian always wanted to please her. I was conflicted and wanted to intervene and insist that Lillian eat inside, but I was too chicken to question my grandmother, just like all the other adults I had never challenged. When Arnie died in 1971, Lillian was at her side, not any other family members—only Lillian.

After I graduated from college and was back home less and less often, I would only see Lillian on holidays. She was always kind, friendly, and made absolutely fabulous rolls! She would go to my parents' houses the day before the holiday to make the dough and to leave it to rise. The next day she would roll out the dough, cut it into circles, dip them in butter, place a circle of dough in a round pan, and then fold it over. She somehow would have hot rolls ready when you first got your plate of food and then would serve hot rolls a couple of times during the meal. The entire family loved Lillian's rolls! Sometimes it was a fight to have the last one, but thankfully she usually made enough to have with the leftovers—that is, if everyone was reasonable in their consumption of rolls—but it was difficult to limit yourself!

I moved back to the Bryan College Station area in March of 1991 when my ex-husband could no longer give me child support and I could not afford to live in Houston any longer. I got a job working for the school district as the drug education coordinator and somehow ended up with administrative hours, thus having to work until five p.m. At the suggestion of my stepmother, I got in touch with Lillian to see what she was doing and if she would be interested in looking after my girls after school. She was delighted and ready to start immediately. She came over to reacquaint herself with the girls and them with her, even though everyone already knew one another. It was nice to be back in touch with Lillian. I think that she had been struggling to make a living at various jobs since my grandmother passed away in 1971. I originally hired her to be at my house when the girls came home from school, but soon she began to pick the girls up from school, bring them home, and fix their dinner. It was great. Lillian didn't want to just take care of my daughters, she really wanted to work, so she would come to my house much earlier in the day to clean our house and wash and iron our clothes. She'd pick up after the girls, make their beds, and just spoiled us all. I told her I could not pay her to come and work the whole day. She understood that, but she was accustomed to working and needed something to do all day—lucky me, lucky us!

I didn't have a lot of money. I was bringing home a little less than two thousand dollars a month and so to give her four hundred of that every month was a stretch for me, but I always felt guilty that I could not pay her more because she was certainly worth more than a hundred dollars a week!

When Lillian came over for the first time for a reintroduction to my girls, she called me "Miss May Sue" (no African American that I know pronounced the "r"), and I told her we needed to drop the "miss." She said she did not know if she could. I suggested that it was certainly not necessary and that it made me uncomfortable. However, most of the time, she called each of us by "miss" and our name; it was a difficult habit to break. One day she looked tired and I asked her to come into the family room and sit down. She said that she did not need to sit. I insisted, but I could tell she was uncomfortable. I acknowledged that she was not accustomed to sitting on the couch with Arnie, but it was now okay to sit on the couch with me. I did not want to stress her, but I did not want there to be separation either.

My girls were very involved in community theater when they were in elementary school and had some lead roles in plays, so they always wanted Lillian, who by now was like another grandmother to them, to come to their performances. I would always have a ticket for her, but the first couple of times she could not make it; I imagine she found it really difficult. I knew that it was hard for her to come to this theater that was predominantly white kids. The day she finally made it, I met her at the entrance to the auditorium and escorted her to the front row to sit next to me. I know that was against everything that she had ever learned or thought, and I doubt she felt safe, but she meant a lot to my girls, and we wanted her to know it. We wanted to treat her like we would a special friend. During intermission, I introduced her as my friend to the director, the stage manager, costume designer, and several actors who all made her to feel welcome. I was aware that I was making her stretch, but I felt it was important to my daughters' upbringing to not have the barriers that I had been raised with when I was growing up. I appreciated her letting down her guard to be more a part of our family by sitting in the front row with me. In my history, we had come a long way—from the "colored" entrance to the theater, to Lillian and me sitting together in the front row. It may not have been particularly comfortable for either of us, but it was necessary. Fading were the days of little white girls having a woman of color look after them, which is great in the evolution of race relationships, but I regret that those special heartfelt relations no longer exist, at least not from my perspective.

Lillian liked to wear a wig when she was out in public. She had some really nice-looking ones, but they made her hot, so when she got to my house to work, she would take her wig off and hang it on the ladder-back chair. A friend from Houston came to visit one weekend and when she saw "something" hanging on the chair, she thought it was a dead animal, and it scared her. We still have a good laugh remembering Lillian's wig!

What I loved the most about Lillian working for us was the display of affection when Lillian left every afternoon, as it was such progress from when Lillian worked for Arnie, my grandmother. Kate would throw her arms around Lillian's neck and say, "A bushel and a peck and a hug around the neck," and give Lillian a hug goodbye. This really was difficult for Lillian at first. I could see that in her face, but Kate continued until Lillian finally became comfortable. It's interesting how all those years of "in your place" training by my grandmother caused so much restriction in Lillian that she could not fully enjoy the hugs for a while, as this kind of touching made her nervous.

It is interesting how race could get in the way of being close. We have much more to overcome than just being able to sit with each other, at least for this generation.

In 1994 I began learning to do energy work, a form of hands on healing, Healing Touch, to be specific, which is a program requiring certification that was first introduced as a holistic nursing program. I enjoyed seeing what results I would get by putting my hands on people, using a few techniques I learned. Lillian had high blood pressure and her feet would swell quite often, which looked very uncomfortable, and was! I asked her one day if I could attempt to offer her some relief for her feet. She was a little hesitant at first, but I convinced her to sit down and let me see if I could help her. She sat in the chair and I sat at her feet. I could tell that her being in the chair and my being on the floor, and at her feet no less, was really difficult for her; it made her anxious and antsy. I quickly began holding her left foot to drain the "fluid." She said that she did not know if she believed in things that she could not see, as that was not how she was raised. I laughed and said that I certainly was not raised to believe in energy work either, but that I knew it worked. We only worked for a few minutes, as it was time for her to get home, but her swelling did begin to subside. She called me later that evening to tell me that all of the swelling was gone and she had no pain for the first time in a long time. She said she did not understand it, but she certainly was enjoying the results of the energy work. I thought about what had happened—not just the energy work, but the fact that our roles had reversed. Even if just for a few minutes, I was serving her. I sat at her feet, and she was above me. The symbolism made me smile, as if it were a transition of the races.

On Saturday, January 2, 1999, Lillian was working at my house, which was unusual for a Saturday. I think she had missed a day earlier in the week and did not want to get behind. I had offered to do energy work on her when she was finished with what she was doing before she left to go home. By this time, we had moved to full-blown treatments on my massage table. I was to go to lunch with a friend who also did energy work and when I got involved with a project with the girls, she offered to work on Lillian, and Lillian and I both agreed. My friend completed the treatment, the girls and I finished our project, and Lillian got up from the table, saying that she felt better. The girls hugged her goodbye and she went home. My friend Sarah and I went to lunch, and during lunch, Sarah shared that Lillian's treatment was unusual as she could not get the lower chakras to open while the crown was wide open, really large. Usually after a treatment, all the chakras are open and spinning clockwise at the same size and rate—at least, that is the goal. We discussed Sarah's results and then moved on to other topics of conversation, still not really understanding about the chakras, until the following day when Lillian's grandson called and told me that Lillian had just passed. I realized then that her crown was open and the lower chakras closed because she was leaving her body. We did not know it at the time or what that meant. I regretted that I had not worked on Lillian that one last time.

Lillian Branch taught me a lot, and I believe that I taught her also. She transformed through the generations from being treated as a suppressed servant kept in her place to an honorary member of our family, sitting on the sofa with my daughters, eating cookies, and watching *The Golden Girls*. Losing Lillian was heartbreaking for all of us. She took such good care of us, brought us such joy, and spoiled us rotten! We all still miss her tremendously and are very grateful that we were a part of her life and she was a part of ours.

Do you have a relationship that has changed dramatically over the years, evolved into a better relationship or role reversal?

My Initiation into Being a Healer

It seems that I was born with health challenges. I write this as an expression of gratitude for my current health and body, even though I have been through the wringer. I remember being an infant, standing in my crib, screaming because my throat hurt and being really hot. This happened a number of times, as I had repeated strep infections. I recall being taken out of my bed and put into cool bathwater in order to lower my temperature. I was put on medication a number of times, too, and made many trips to the doctor. I remember being taken to Fort Worth to see a children's doctor, since my mother was from Fort Worth, and being told that I needed to have my tonsils out, but at that time, they did not do tonsillectomies until a child was age five or older.

So, sometime around my fifth birthday, I remember being fed toast, applesauce, and mushy foods. Great care was being taken around my health to make sure that I didn't get sick so that I could go to Fort Worth and have my tonsils out. I remember checking into the hospital, which was a busy place, and getting a room. It was an eerie feeling, and I was scared. My mother was with me. She stayed in the hospital with me, but it was just kind of creepy to be around so many sick children.

I remember being taken into the operating room and looking up at a big light, and all of a sudden, there was this cone-like thing coming over my face. I inhaled, and it felt like porcupine quills were shooting into my nose. And then I don't remember anything until I woke up in my room hours later. It seems like I stayed in the hospital a long time, and that my father made a trip to town to take my mother out to dinner. While they were gone, I panicked. I felt abandoned. What if they did not come back? I was in this strange place by myself. I'd gotten to know some of the nurses and I had seen some of the children, but I don't think I'd had much interaction with them.

I cried to the nurse so much that she called the restaurant where my parents were eating to tell them I was upset, and they came back. I'm sure that didn't please my dad too much, but I was glad that my mom was back with me. I do remember that the nurses would come in often and take my temperature. I don't recall if I ever had a temperature; I just remember that it was with a rectal thermometer and how much I hated it. And I don't know if they bribed me or if I wouldn't cooperate, but after every temperature-taking, I got rewarded with a Popsicle, which I really liked.

Again, I'm not sure how long I was at the hospital. It seems like at least a week, maybe longer. I do remember that when we left the hospital, it was a bright, sunny day and I was in the front seat in my pajamas and robe, with my mom driving us home. Once we were on the outskirts of Fort Worth, she stopped for gas, and the gas station attendant checked the oil under the hood. We started out again, got on the freeway, and we were on a high part on the freeway, an overpass area, when all of a sudden, the hood of the station wagon flew up, and my mother couldn't see, which was very frightening to both of us. She pulled over as best she could, but there wasn't really much of a shoulder, and she stopped the car. (To this day, I believe I have a body memory of that terror as I do not like freeways and especially overpasses.)

She realized that she needed to get out of the car to close the hood. When the wind had blown the hood up, it had been pushed at such an angle that she wasn't able to push it down by herself. My mom got back in the car and told me that she was going to have to go find help. This was 1955 and there wasn't a whole lot of traffic on the freeway, as it was mid-morning. Somehow or another, Mama made it to a boat business on the feeder street below that we could see from where we were parked on the overpass. I believe that they sold motorboats.

I had to sit in the car by myself, hoping that my mother would come back, that nobody would come get me while she was gone, and that she would be able to bring somebody back to help us, which she did. Fortunately, a man from the boat business brought my mother back in his car, along with some tools and materials to get the hood back down and closed tight. The gentleman wired the hood to the body of the car, as the latch was broken and he wanted to be sure that it didn't fly up again. Apparently, when the man at the service station had checked our oil, he had not closed the hood tightly and when the wind got under the hood as we reached the top of the overpass, it blew it open. Once the hood was secured, we were on our way, but it was a scary hour or so sitting on the freeway by myself, waiting for my mom to return after that huge terror that we both felt when the hood flew up.

We made it back home safely and after that, health-wise, life was just sniffles and sneezes. No more horrible strep throat!

My next big health crisis was when I would get aches and pains in my joints. My mother took me to our family doctor, who ran some tests, which did not show that there was anything wrong. He said he thought that I was just making it up, that I was a hypochondriac. Maybe I was, I don't know, but I do know that I had terrible pains in my wrists, elbows, and knees. I kept having these aching joints and feeling lousy overall. Mama could tell I felt bad. I mean, when I felt bad, I felt bad, and my mom knew it, but our family doctor kept saying nothing was wrong with me. Finally, one night, I started having chest pains. I remember it was close to bedtime. The complaint of chest pains really frightened Mama, so she called a female doctor in town who would make house calls; she came over right away and listened to my heart to check me out. I think that as a result of this incident, my mother decided that she needed to have me examined by someone other than our family doctor.

We needed to have a second opinion about why I was having all these aches and why I now had this pain in my chest. I was only seven.

My grandmother had a dear friend named Dr. Charlie Stone, who was a professor at the UT Medical branch in Galveston. He had grown up with her in Caldwell, and he was a very good doctor. My mother decided to take me to see Dr. Stone, who became kind of like a grandfather to me, as my grandfather had died in 1954, and this was 1957. I loved to watch Dr. Stone read things, and I loved to watch him write his notes. He wrote all his notes on little cards. He was a short little bald man, who wore round wire glasses. He was always rubbing his lips back and forth together as he was writing or as he was reading a report.

Dr. Stone had a number of tests run on me. I remember I had to go to two places to have blood drawn, which I absolutely hated. I also had an EKG, which, back in 1957, took forever and you had to have these little suction cups put all over your chest with a cold, slippery cream. Then the machine was run by Dr. Stone's nurse, Miss Ferguson, who was one of those people who was always cranky, but I knew she liked me and my intuition told me when to talk and when to be quiet. After each EKG, Dr. Stone would call us in to his office and he would review all of the test results and share the results with my mom and me. He got the test results pretty quickly as we never stayed in Galveston more than a few days when going for an appointment with Dr. Stone.

His office was in the Moody Building, which was in downtown Galveston. It had an elevator and I got to push the button to go up and down. His office was not fancy at all; it had lots of mismatched chairs in the waiting area, some with arm rests and others without, and there were lots of people. Sometimes we had to wait a very long time to see him, so long that my mother always took her sewing to help pass the time. He was worth the wait, as he didn't have a fifteen-minute rule. He would visit with every patient for as long as necessary, but you had to be willing to wait your turn.

I remember my initial visit, going in and Dr. Stone reading through all the tests, and then looking at my mother and talking to her, telling her that I had rheumatic fever and it was the worst case of rheumatic fever he had ever seen or heard of, but it had caused the least amount of heart damage. So he and my mother talked. He said that I needed to be taking penicillin, and they talked about what that would mean and how I would take it and how often. I remember thinking they sounded very grim, and I really didn't understand it. I couldn't wait to get out of his office and to the elevator to ask Mama if I was going to die.

Mama looked at me and took my hand. She kind of smiled and said, "No, no. You're not going to die. You are sick, you have an illness, but you can take medicine for it."

She was very reassuring, and so I felt much better after our chat. I felt much better about the illness, too … until I had my first penicillin shot. I was a seven-year-old child when I got the shot. It seemed like it was a huge tube of medication, and it hurt entering my body, causing a raised, hot welt. I didn't like shots or needles to begin with, but then to add the painful medication was almost more than I could stand. Then, after the shot, my arm or hip, depending on where the shot was given, became very swollen, hot, and inflamed. Fortunately, or unfortunately for me, after I had the second shot, I broke out in horrific hives all over my body and I had shortness of breath. Mama called the doctor immediately. He told her to put me in a cold bath of something to try to calm the hives down, and then to put calamine lotion all over me, so that I wouldn't itch. And then I got a high fever.

I was supposed to spend the night with a friend that night. I think she may have come to my house to distract me from how bad I felt, but this was my reaction to penicillin. After that, the doctor was afraid for me to have it because I'd had such a reaction. Dr. Stone had a second choice for medication, which I took, and I believe that it was a capsule. I took it for a couple of days, and every time I took it, I threw it up, so that one didn't work either. We moved on to the third and last medication choice, which I remember Dr. Stone saying was the least effective.

He was concerned about my health, and he wanted me to take this sulfa drug twice a day, and he wanted me to take it for ten years, until I was seventeen.

Fortunately, I didn't have a reaction to this one, or at least none that I'm aware of. I didn't throw up—I could keep it down—and I didn't break out in hives or have a fever. I was also glad that I didn't have to take that penicillin shot because my mother had begun to talk to me about giving myself the shot. I had a big mental picture of that at age seven, knowing how much I hated needles and how much the shot hurt, and I didn't see how I was ever going to convince myself to do that. I had ended up with the third medication, the sulfa-based drug, and so I was taking it. As the doctor instructed, I took it religiously until I was seventeen, shortly before I went off to college.

I did have some health issues after my mother died in 1964. I dealt with a lot of depression. I took something, but I don't know what I took. I think it was probably an antidepressant. I drank a lot of tea in the afternoon, which the housekeeper told me was probably the reason that I couldn't sleep at night. But I wouldn't admit that because I really liked the tea and, as a teenager, I could not admit that I was wrong.

In May of my senior year in high school, I started trembling and losing weight, feeling very anxious. It was mid-May and we were graduating May 30th. My parents took me to the doctor and, after some tests, found out that I had hyperthyroid issues, so I was prescribed thyroid medication just before I graduated from high school. I learned later how stress can activate illnesses, and I guess maybe it was the stress of graduating from from high school that began my thyroid issues.

I had all these cute little dresses to wear to graduation parties, but hyperthyroidism had caused me to lose so much weight that the dresses didn't fit quite as well as they had when we purchased them. Then, after graduation, we started planning my move to Austin to attend the University of Texas and going through Rush, so we were buying fall clothes for me to wear to Rush, which is a series of parties at sorority houses to see which one you would like to join and who would like you as a member. My Rush clothes were a smaller size than the ones I had for graduation, as I had not regained the weight lost before graduation. During that summer, from June to September, I gained between thirty and forty pounds. The week before Rush, I gained ten pounds without putting a bite of food in my mouth and survived only on water. The hyperthyroid medication that I had been taking to slow my thyroid down had done just that, so I went back to the doctor for another test and the doctor discovered that my thyroid had gone completely the other direction into hypothyroidism. And that's why I felt so lethargic, depressed, and had gained so much weight without eating anything. My meds were then changed to treat hypothyroid disease.

So I went off to the University of Texas with thyroid problems, about twenty-five or thirty pounds heavier than I had weighed at the end of high school, and with another new wardrobe, as the clothes that were previously bought for Rush no longer fit. I did not have my usual body weight and therefore lacked confidence and just did not feel well.

I was now taking thyroid medicine for hypothyroid, but since I had turned seventeen, I no longer needed to take those chalky white tablets that I'd been taking twice a day every day for ten years, so I stopped taking them. No one told me to slowly wean off these meds; I just stopped abruptly.

Shortly after I got to college, I suddenly started having kidney and yeast infections. This was before people realized exactly what antibiotics did to your body. I did not realize that the sulfa-based drug that I had been taking was a sulfa-based antibiotic. I don't know why I never put the two of those together until about age forty-five. I always thought the drug was a sulfa drug. My mother had died when I was thirteen, so there wasn't really anybody keeping good track of my medication or my health. And all of a sudden, I was experiencing what happens to you when you get off a long-term antibiotic, having massive outbreaks of candida and kidney infections. I had so many kidney infections that I ended up having an exploratory surgery during spring break my freshman year to make sure that, indeed, my kidneys were okay, and they were. But I believe that, because of taking the sulfa-based antibiotic for so long, I had systemic candida.

During my freshman year, I was taking thyroid medication for being hypothyroid. It seemed like I'd begun to lose the weight I had gained, but I started having trouble with my eyes. By 1971, the summer between my junior and senior years in college, Dr. Stone, my Galveston doctor, recommended that I go visit a very special doctor in New York City to see what was going on with my eyes. My stepmother and I went to New York to see the highly recommended doctor, who thought that I had an inflammation behind my eyes, so he put me on steroids. This was in June. I started taking massive doses of steroids, which had many side effects, such as retaining a lot of fluid. Because of the fluid retention, I was given a very strong diuretic called Lasix. The Lasix was very effective—so effective that I was losing too much potassium and I began to have severe cramps in all of my muscles, especially my legs. A potassium fizzy drink was added to my pill-taking ritual, and it did help relieve the cramping.

Toward the end of the summer, I started feeling really bad. I woke up my roommate one morning to go to class and she sat up and looked at me and said, "Oh my God. What happened to you?" Overnight my face had swollen so badly that it had become a "moon" face. The bones in my legs felt like they were disintegrating. I felt just awful. I had been taking all of my prescriptions: twenty prednisone tablets divided into four doses daily plus two Lasix, one in the morning and one in the evening, and the potassium drink in the morning. I felt so bad that I didn't think I could walk, but I knew one of my roommates had some Darvon, so I crawled into her bathroom and took some of it to get rid of the cramps. The Darvon did not help, so I took some aspirin. I think I was offered and took more over-the-counter drugs to try to feel better, but nothing worked. Before the day was over, my roommates and the six guys who lived down the hall took me to the ER. Now, you have to remember this was 1971. Street drugs were rampant in Austin, Texas. But I was taking pharmaceuticals, not the kind of street drugs that the ER staff thought I had been taking. I will say we were kind of a motley-looking crew. I'd been feeling bad all day and it was summertime. Everybody had on T-shirts, cut-offs and flip-flops, probably uncombed hair, and they'd been staring at me all day. The hospital staff asked me lots of questions, tested me, and found out that, indeed, I was not taking any illicit drugs, but they had no recommendations for relieving my pain or suggestions about what I was taking other than discussing it with my doctor.

I called Dr. Stone, who had sent me to New York, but his son was now taking over his practice, so I had to work with him. I told him I was never going to take another prednisone and he told me that I couldn't do that, because it would kill me if I stopped taking it abruptly. He gave me a plan to slowly wean off the meds. It was going to take me until the end of October to safely get off the prednisone. I took prednisone from June to October; my eyes did not get any better and the rest of my body suffered. The good news was that because I looked so bad with my moon face, I got to miss Rush without paying a fine. The gals in charge of Rush were glad that I was not there. I felt terrible, I looked terrible, I wasn't wanted during Rush, and I probably physically could not have done it. On a humorous note, my roommates and I always gave each other birthday presents, usually whatever the current fad item was. Well, the current fad was makeup mirrors, so they gave me a makeup mirror for my birthday. It even had lights. Just what I wanted, to be able to look at my big old moon face in this lighted makeup mirror. How ironic.

That fall, during my senior year, my suite mate was a pharmacy major and they were studying steroids in her pharmacy class. She'd come home and say, "Oh, you don't have this side effect." And she would tell me about it and I would go, "Oh, yes, I do." I think I had every side effect there was, at least every one that she shared with me. I did not even realize all of the things that were happening until she mentioned them, such as fuzzy hair on my face, to name one.

At the end of October, I had finally weaned off the prednisone. My boyfriend at the time took a picture of me taking my last pill. I slowly began to feel better and the side effects began to subside.

I graduated from college and began teaching school, where I acquired every bacteria, virus, or whatever disease was going around among the elementary school students that I taught. I used more than my ten sick days my first year of teaching because I caught every illness that any of my students had.

Fortunately for me, my immunity built up and in time I no longer caught my students' illnesses.

In 1972, I was referred to an eye doctor at Baylor in Houston. He was relatively new to Baylor, young and highly thought of. I went to him for an examination, primarily because of droopy eyelids and the fact that my eyes did not track together. The steroids had not worked. I told him about my thyroid issues, and he believed that that was probably the reason for my eye problems. The first surgery that he suggested doing was to open my eyes by lifting my lids, since they were sagging. I had that surgery in the summer and it was successful, as my eyes were more open. He did the stitches underneath, which was kind of irritating and felt like I had sand in my eyes for a little while until the stitches melted. I did like the way my eyes were more open, and I had a greater range of vision.

Then the next year, I had another eye surgery for tracking, but it was not as successful. I had a frightening experience while waiting my turn.

The doctor had run into a problem with the surgery before mine, so I was having to wait. I remember being in a hallway, with others lined up on gurneys like I was, all waiting our turn for a surgery. I had a tag on my gurney and my wrist. I had been given something to keep me relaxed so I was not anxious, and I could hear things going on but

I could not move or talk. Two medical techs came in the hallway and were moving people around. They grabbed my gurney and put me on the elevator. We were going up, up somewhere, and I guessed they were finally taking me up for surgery. I heard them chatting away about something when all of a sudden, one of them looked down and went, "Oh my gosh, we got the wrong patient!" This statement scared me, and I was afraid of where they might be taking me. I had heard of people having the wrong surgery. I remember thinking, *What if I am taken in for a hysterectomy? What should I do?*

All of a sudden, I was trying my best to speak, trying to move, but fight as I might, I was suddenly completely out. I didn't hear anything else. When I woke up, I remembered the words of the techs and I felt my eye and realized that yes, indeed, I did have eye surgery. Fortunately, they had realized their mistake and I assume had returned me to the hallway and gotten the right patient. But that was pretty scary. That was my first eye muscle surgery. It was somewhat successful. Then, a couple years later, in 1975, I had eye surgery again on the other eye. I was married. My husband at the time dropped me off at the hospital. My parents came to town to sit with me and to be at the hospital with me, which was probably a good thing because my husband went to work. My parents were a little upset that my husband wasn't there because he actually was the next of kin. On this particular eye surgery, I was the first patient in the morning, which ended up being very fortunate for me in that the doctor operated on me and that's when the medical center flooded, the power went out, and the elevators stopped running. I don't remember how many floors my parents had to climb to come up to see me, but they did and they helped to get me home. Each eye muscle surgery was a little successful, but not like what I wanted or expected.

I had another eye muscle surgery in 1978. These surgeries were for the muscles behind my eyes to get my eyes to track together. I had two surgeries on one eye and one surgery on the other. In 1993, I had another eyelid surgery. For this one, I'm not sure what the doctor was doing in that the stitches were on the outside. You could see the scar. He wanted to make it look like my eyes were open, but my eyelids were all lumpy from where the stitches were and where fluid would build up, and they really looked bad. After that particular surgery, I started having really watery eyes, especially the left one. I went back to the doctor and found out that I had what's called dry eye. Dry eye makes your eyes water, but it doesn't lubricate your eye with the proper moisture. At night I put Saran wrap over my left eye as it doesn't completely close. I am also wearing sclera lenses, which are lenses that you fill with water before putting them on.

In addition to the Saran wrap I put over my eye at night, I wear an eye mask. I have been investigating and have had stem cell treatments to try and help my eyes. I will say that the stem cells have helped with scar tissue, as the scars that I had on my eyes before are much better. My eyelids are no longer lumpy from where stitches were, so I do know that it's helped the scar tissue at least on my eyelids, and I hope it's helped on the back of my eyes. I went to another eye doctor about the possibility of surgery, and he said that he wanted to do a test on me before he did anything to my eyelids. He wanted to make sure that it wasn't a neurological problem. I had to stay in the hospital for four days to have all these neurological tests, which I did. I will say they were very painful, which is a good thing, because I could feel my muscles. I was being tested for myasthenia gravis. I fortunately did not have myasthenia gravis, but I have something similar to it that just affects my eyes. It's a chronic progressive external ophthalmoplegia (CPEO) deterioration of the ability of the muscles to hold my eyes open or to track together. I have not had another surgery on my eyes for years just because I never felt like anything was successful, but it's come to the point that it's necessary, so I'm going to try again. I'm going to bite the bullet and have my lids opened.

I have to be very careful about what pharmaceuticals I take, as I am too sensitive and my body overreacts.

Pharmaceuticals and I don't agree, so I take a lot of food-type supplements and some vitamins. I take a compounded thyroid, and I use bioidentical hormones, which all help me. I'm very grateful to my body with all the drugs that I've exposed it to, especially the penicillin and steroids. I am very appreciative of my body, that it is still moving at sixty-eight. I may not be as healthy as I would like to be, but I do work on it. I support people in taking an interest in their own health, and finding out about their lab work and other test results. It is your body and your lab work. To me, keeping track of medical test results yourself is important because, if a doctor gives you fifteen minutes, that's not a very long time to understand what might be going on with you.

I realize that seeing a specialist may not be helpful because the whole body needs to be considered, as nothing operates independently. Everything in our body works together. I really try and be mindful of that, and if I have an imbalance, I think about how it's affecting the rest of my body and what I can do to be back in balance.

Because of my track record with doctors and drugs, I became interested in alternative medicine and especially energy work, such as hands on healing. I have found that some of the ancient healing modalities are very effective and are now making their way into mainstream medicine in America!

I enjoy energy work so much that I became a practitioner. I first learned Reiki and then Healing Touch, as Healing Touch was a medical model, created by a nurse. I have studied several other energy programs, but so far I like Healing Touch the most. I am currently in a new program and am learning some skills that I missed in HT. Energy work is mysterious, as you cannot "see" it, but it can be felt, if not at the time, then after the healing sessions are complete. Energy will go where it needs to go, and sometimes it is surprising what happens in a session. Once I was guided to hold my hands on the shoulder of a woman at the end of our session. I did not know why, but I did it and after the session while we were talking I told her what I had done. She said it was probably because she had not been able to lift her arm to hang up her son's shirts. She was shocked that she had lifted her arm and she could now hold it up! I was surprised also, but grateful that the energy had helped to improve her range of motion in that arm.

I love many different types of alternative healing, and I look forward to these modalities becoming mainstream. Craniosacral, lymphatic drainage, massage, acupuncture, and IV therapy have all been beneficial to me. Another treatment that I have done and I look forward to becoming more reasonably priced is stem cell treatments. After I have a treatment, I feel wonderful for weeks! The type of stem cell treatments that I've had were non-invasive, using my own blood, which was enhanced after spinning the blood to harvest the healing cells. One of the things that I really noticed after a treatment was the melting of scar tissue. I had a terrible time with scar tissue, as three incisions had been made in the same place. The scar was thick and ropey and there was so much of it, it caused my hip to be rotated. After my first treatment, I noticed that when I stretched out on the bed, there was no longer a pulling sensation. It's not that I had even noticed a pulling before, but I suddenly noticed the absence of pulling. I also realized that I could stand up straighter and the scars on my eyelids disappeared. I feel that stem cells are the future of medicine, and I cannot wait for them to be more affordable and used more widely!

Here's to better and better health. I look forward to new technologies, stem cell research, and a way to assist our bodies in healing themselves. I do know that within us, our bodies know what they need. If we just listen and pay attention, our bodies can guide us in taking the right steps toward being healthier.

Does your body have a message for you?

The Trauma of Losing My Mother

On June 19, 2018, fifty-four years after the death of my mother, I finally linked the word "trauma" with that event. Not only was her actual death a trauma, but so were the months afterwards—for a long time, actually. When did it end, or has it? I realized that it was a loss, and I experienced grief from that loss, but I never considered it a trauma until the summer of 2018.

I was close to my mother, whom I called Mama. I spent lots of time with her and I knew what her medical ailments were and what she took for each one. Mama made fabulous clothes for me. She would see something she liked and she would copy it. She was a talented seamstress! She wanted me to sew and was even encouraging me to do so from her deathbed. I tried it, but once I completed a sewing project, I no longer liked it or wanted to wear it. I am the same with cooking. Once it's cooked, I'm done with it. I do not want to eat it.

My mother was very active in the community. She was involved in my siblings' school events and our church. I know that she was the Den Mother for my brother's Boy Scout troop, and I believe that she helped with Girl Scouts. She not only loved to sew, but she also loved to play bridge on a regular basis. And she LOVED to drink coffee. She often entertained friends in our home and was a gracious hostess who threw lavish dinner parties.

I will admit that I was a spoiled child, and I probably am still spoiled as an adult. I guess my mother is the one who did the spoiling. My dad worked long hours so my time with him was limited. Mama took me on trips with her and her friends, which was fun for me instead of being left at home with Rodee, even though I loved spending time with Rodee, too. Sometimes Mama would go shopping in Houston with a friend and she would not take me, but she would ask what I wanted her to bring back for me. A day trip to Houston and I could have asked for anything, probably even a new Tiny Tears, my favorite doll, but no, what I wanted were Band-Aids. For some reason I had a love for Band-Aids, probably because I had to be bleeding in order to have one. Otherwise, I had to let any wound "air out." I did not like the fancy or themed ones, only the plain ones. I liked Band-Aids so much that my personalized Christmas stocking had a box of Band-Aids pictured on it.

Mama was thoughtful of my feelings and tried to prevent problems before they happened. I always wanted to sleep with my parents, or I should say that I wanted to sleep with Mama. When my siblings were away at camp during the summer, my mother had a youth bed put in their bedroom so that I could be in the same room with them, since the rest of the bedrooms were empty. It was a big house with big rooms and fourteen-foot ceilings. I was accustomed to sleeping in the room with my two older sisters, so I would get really lonesome.

Mama became ill in the sixties, when people did not talk about death or cancer. My mother had many other ailments she talked about, but not cancer. It was a frightening time for me when she was ill. It all started in the fall of 1961. I came home for lunch during the early part of the school year, and Mama told me she had discovered a lump in her breast about the size of an olive. She had seen our family doctor, and she was leaving for Houston that afternoon to have surgery to have the lump removed. She told me about the lump at lunch and was gone by the time I got home from school, which was upsetting. I did not understand the emergency. My brother and I were the only ones living at home, as my older sisters were away at college. Mrs. Rawls, who worked at our church, came and stayed with my brother and me as my dad was going to take my mom to Houston. He stayed in Houston at the Tideway Motel, right by the medical center. I went on with my life, going to school and coming home. I do not remember being particularly worried until the evening after the surgery when Mrs. Rawls announced that my dad had called and said that my mother was fine.

I got a flash: "No, she is not fine, she has lung cancer," I said, not knowing where those words or ideas came from. I said this out loud to Mrs. Rawls, and she tried to dismiss my statement and tell me that was not correct, and that she was fine.

Mama was in Houston in the hospital for what seemed like a really long time, as this was before time limits on hospital stays. I believe that she was in the hospital for over two weeks. Family friends went to Houston to visit her and would tell me about their visits, but I never got to go, as children did not visit hospitals much in those days! My dad was with her until she came home, which must have been on a Saturday, because I was at home. When she arrived home, she went to bed and stayed there for several more days. I remember she had all of this tape around her chest and as I was just beginning to develop breasts myself, I knew that if her boobs were pressed that tightly against her chest, it would hurt, so I asked her about it. She explained that there was no breast there anymore on her right side, that it had been removed, along with a number of lymph glands. The incision went way up under her collarbone. She explained that the doctor had made the incision and peeled back her skin and had taken everything, while I had been thinking that they had taken the "lump the size of an olive." Since the surgery was so invasive, it took her a while to resume her physical duties, but I was sure glad to have her home.

Mama was sick, or she had been sick, and no one was talking about it, not even her! I felt alone, as I usually did, being the youngest, with five years between my next sibling and myself. I always thought of my parents and my siblings as the family that I was observing, always trying to join. I was on the outside, looking in.

I believe that my mom wanted to hurry up and get her strength back, as my oldest sister, Angela, was making her debut in Fort Worth, where Mama grew up and where she had made her debut. It would be "old home" time for my mother, as she would get to see lots of friends and relatives from Fort Worth at the many events planned for the fall. Mama had a beautiful evening gown made for herself to wear to my sister's presentation. The top had to be remade to fit my mother's new torso, which had a huge scar and indention around her collarbone. She looked lovely, even though she was still a bit weak from her surgery.

I am uncertain of the exact sequence of events for her after that, but I do remember the events that impacted me the most. I recollect her going back and forth to Houston after the surgery to have radiation, or what she called "cobalt" treatments, but I am not certain when that started. My guess is that it started after she recovered from the surgery. The person giving the radiation in Houston had drawn on her chest with a black marker, and she said the marks indicated where to give her the radiation treatment. I must admit that was a little unnerving! I felt off-balance during this time, as my mom was not fully present anymore and was making many trips to Houston; they were usually just day trips, but still, she wasn't at home. I did not fully realize the seriousness of her illness until December of 1963. My parents went to Houston for the day for Mama to have a checkup. You see, they went for the day because that night was the Woman's Club annual Christmas formal and Mama would be there for that, to help me get dressed. After all, this was only my second such event, and these dances only came around once a year. When I got home from school, my older sister Angela, whom I was not very close to at the time, as she was married by then and had a one-year-old daughter, was at our family home. Mother and Daddy would not be home in time to see me off to my formal, and they might not be home until the next day, as Mama had a report from the Houston doctor that she had a spot on her lungs. This had obviously scared her and she and my dad were going to Galveston to see Dr. Stone, the doctor we all went to when no other doctor knew the answer to what was wrong. He is the doctor who diagnosed me with rheumatic fever, as mentioned previously. A spot showed up on her x-ray and she wanted Dr. Stone to determine if it was scar tissue from the surgery and radiation or if it was another cancer spot. Not only was I devastated by her news, I was crushed that she would not be there to help me dress and to see me off on my big "growing up" event and take my picture. It was a horrible feeling, one that I would get to know quite well; it was a terrible, gnawing feeling that became a part of me, one I hated but that was so familiar, it would not go away and leave me alone. I'm sorry, but it is not the same to have your older sister with you instead of your mother when you are about to go on your "second date." I remember seeing one picture of me before I went out that evening in my shiny coral dress. I have that look of a deer in the headlights, but I do have a smile on my face. This event was probably the real attachment of the "mask" that I would wear for many years. "Stand there and look pretty" was taking over in my relationship to my mother and her health, not just to other things that I did not need to worry about.

For the Christmas of 1963, the last one we would have with Mama, the family went to Houston and spent the night at the Rice Hotel and went shopping, buying our own Christmas presents as my mom had not felt up to shopping for us. It was a fun time in my book—staying in a hotel, going out to fancy dinners and shopping, buying clothes and just being with my family. I did not realize just how strange this was until I was older. We spent Christmas Day with our extended family, aunts, uncles, and cousins who lived in our area, but we had done all our shopping for ourselves. I went along, my oblivious self, not really paying a lot of attention to my mom and her health, at least if I could avoid thinking about it. There were subtle incidents that I thought were a little odd, but I dismissed them. I did not want anything to be wrong, so I denied any obvious strangeness.

Mama had always wanted to go to the Holy Land, so in the spring of 1964, my parents and another couple from Bryan went on a cruise to the Holy Land. My oldest sister, brother-in-law, and their daughter came to stay at my parents' home while my parents were away for about six weeks. My mom was losing her hair, which concerned her. She met a woman on the cruise who told her about a hairstylist in New York City who could make her a natural-looking hair piece if she would stay in NYC to meet him, which she decided to do. The new hairpiece was very attractive and made my mom feel better about how she looked, but I had hoped that she would be home sooner.

The beginning of the most horrifying events started in the early summer of 1964. Aunt Jane and her husband Jim came to visit us, which they did at least once a year, usually on their way to Mexico, where my uncle liked to go deep-sea fishing. They would always drive their big black Lincoln Continental all the way from Oklahoma to the coast of Mexico. I am not sure how the arrangements were made, but while Jane was in town, Mama decided that we needed to make a trip to Houston, as we usually went to Houston to shop for clothes of the season twice a year, once in the spring/summer and again in the fall/ winter. So Mama, Jane, and I went to Houston. We stayed once again at the Rice Hotel. I was excited; growing up and being more interested in clothes, I thought that this would be fun, shopping with my mom and my aunt! My excitement was crushed when Mama spent most of the night coughing. I was irritated because her constant, persistent coughing kept us all awake and left her too exhausted to shop the next day. Prior to our trip, my Aunt Jane had made plans to visit Houston friends, so she was not around during the day. Since my mom was too tired to shop, she sent me out alone at age thirteen, which was not such a big deal at that time. Bank cards were not in existence yet, but stores allowed you to take things home "on approval," which is what I did. We discussed what I needed. She told me to pick out what I liked, try it on to see if it fit, and bring the clothes back to the hotel to model for her. I would return what we decided not to keep. When we did our yearly shopping, we bought a lot of clothes, as this would be for the entire season, so we had to buy casual clothes, church clothes, and school clothes. I wish I had taken a picture of the sales ladies' faces when I told them that I wanted to charge all of those clothes. One of the clerks actually called my mom in her hotel room to make sure that I was supposed to be purchasing all of them. My mom did have accounts at Foley's, Sakowitz and Neiman Marcus, where I was shopping, but this was still unusual. I was uncomfortable being questioned, shopping alone, and then taking all of the clothes across the street to the hotel. When sent out to shop, I was given a few specific things to look for, like a dark suit for Sunday school, some shorts, sundresses, and some school clothes for the opening weeks of school. I remember buying a navy suit, a skirt with a jacket, and a blue-and-white-striped knit top that went with the suit. I can still see the suit and feel the fabric, as that was what I wore to my mom's funeral exactly a week later. I suppose that her instruction to select something dark was to be sure I would look nice for her funeral. I also remember a cute white sundress with a watermelon on it, and then there was the culotte outfit that I wore when I tried out for the cheerleading squad later that fall. I took the mounds of clothes to the hotel, tried them on, and then returned what we did not need before the end of the day. I realized that my mom was not very healthy, but I did not realize how sick she was. We went home on Saturday, the night that my parents usually went out to the Country Club. I think my dad cooked steaks at home that night as Mama was too tired, and I modeled clothes for my dad, Uncle Jim and Aunt Jane. Jane and Jim were going to leave for Mexico the next morning. I was sad to see them go, as we loved their visits because they were so fun and entertaining!

On the Monday after our shopping trip my mom stayed in bed pretty much all day, with the exception of an hour or so when my sister Angela took her to the doctor. I think she was exhausted from our trip to Houston. I was on the phone with my then-boyfriend when an oxygen tank was delivered upstairs to her bedroom. I wondered about that, but then I realized that she was using it because she was having trouble breathing. That day was my dad's birthday, but we did not have a big celebration planned, as Mother was not up to it. While I was on the phone with my boyfriend, I became aware that I had completely forgotten his birthday; it had been on the eleventh, four days before. I was really embarrassed but I know now that I was more preoccupied with Mama than I realized. I shared with my mom that I had forgotten his birthday and she suggested calling the print shop and ordering him some personalized stationary, which I did. I ordered paper and envelopes with his initials, no periods, and address. I was not thinking clearly and when I went to pick up the stationary, at the top of the letter-writing paper was the word "TAP". It took me a minute, but I realized that without the periods, his initials did spell "TAP".

The day went on, and I had a sick feeling. Daddy came home and Mama came downstairs for daddy's birthday dinner; she was dressed. I have a picture of her; she looks bad, but I realized later that as a person looks worse, you don't necessarily realize it if you see them every day, especially if you are in denial. We ate dinner, had some cake, and my mom went back upstairs to bed. My dad went up with her and about an hour later my dad was frantically yelling down the stairs at me, which he never did, to bring my mom's meds. I couldn't understand him and went running halfway up the stairs to ask him what he was saying. He was frustrated that I did not have the meds with me. I ran back down and got them, handed them to my dad at the top of the stairs and, for some reason, I went back downstairs. A few minutes later, Daddy let me know that an ambulance was coming to take Mama to the hospital. This did not sound good. The ambulance pulled in the driveway, and the guys with the gurney went in the side door of the house off the porch. They went up the front stairs, as the enclosed back stairs were not large enough for the gurney. I do not remember seeing my mother, except at a distance. I did not go over and look her in the eye and tell her goodbye or that I loved her or anything. I think I was in shock, and

I know I was scared. If I didn't talk with her maybe everything would be okay. Mama could not be sick; she would have told me. She always told me about her health. I do not know where I disappeared to until it was time for my dad and me to get in the car and follow the ambulance to the hospital. I sat alone in the lobby of the hospital that evening for about an hour as I wasn't allowed to go with my dad. My aunt and uncle, who lived in town, showed up about the time Daddy appeared, asking my dad what they could do. Daddy said he would call Jane and Jim to come back. I knew something bad was up as they had just left our house the day before.

I did not see Mama again that night. Daddy and I rode home in silence. After he called Aunt Jane and told her that my mom was in the hospital, he hung up the phone, and I asked him when Mama would get to come home. He said that she probably would not come home, at least not alive. That's how I found out Mama was dying. I was stunned. This could not be happening—not to me. Mama would not leave me; she would tell me if she was going to leave me. I could not believe that no one talked about her being sick; that she did not talk about being sick. This was all a mistake, a bad dream, and I would wake up soon.

This all happened on June 15, 1964, the night of my dad's fifty-second birthday. I was scared. I felt abandoned and alone, a feeling that would become a bad friend, one that I wanted to leave but it would not. I had felt alone at various times in my life. It was a miserable night for both my dad and myself. I slept in my mother's place in their bed, as I did not want to be alone and I do not think Daddy did either. I knew that my mom and dad held hands every night in bed, so I held his hand. I asked him about the hand-holding many years later and he shared with me that he and his closest brother had held hands every night when they were growing up so that gave him a safe, secure feeling.

I am not sure what happened the next day, except that the cloud that I felt all around me seemed heavier. I am pretty sure that Daddy went to The Bottom to work, at least for a while. I wanted to go to the hospital to see Mama, but Daddy told me that my mom did not want me to come to the hospital, as she wanted me to remember her the way she was, not as someone sick in the hospital.

I was miserable. I could not yet drive and did not know what to do. It did not seem right to call my girlfriends and say, *Guess what, my mother is in the hospital dying.* I did not have to do anything, as this small town took care of the news. I think that the entire town knew by sundown on Tuesday that she was in the hospital. I believe that many of them knew that she was dying long before I did. I guess one of my mom's friends felt sorry for me and invited me to go downtown shopping with her and her daughter, who was a friend of mine. I insisted on leaving downtown and walking to the nearby hospital to see Mama, and my friend went with me. Hospitals at that time had visiting hours and the time that we were there was not the "visiting" time, so we snuck in the back door and somehow found my mom's room. She looked very peaceful even though she was having trouble breathing. She usually wore her hair up in a French roll but that day it was down and flowing around her shoulders. My friend commented on how pretty her hair was and that she had never seen it down. Mama did not say much but just smiled and said that we should not be in the hospital when it was not visiting hours.

I got to see Mama every day during her stay, but just for a short time. Again, I was not driving yet so I had to find someone to take me, and most of the family did not think I should witness what was happening. My sister Angela spent most of her day at the hospital with her. My other sister, Patty, who was in Austin in summer school, as was my brother, came home on Wednesday. I went to the hospital with Patty on Friday afternoon to remove some of the flowers in Mama's room because there were so many that you could hardly get in the door. We filled up the back of Mama's station wagon and took them to our house.

On Friday evening one of my friends had a party at her house and, as a teenager in denial, I went. I could not miss a party. I remember telling my boyfriend at the time that my mother was dying. How do you answer that statement? I do not think that he did, but he did not run away from me. When I got home after the party, my Aunt Ellyn, who was married to my mom's brother, had arrived in town and was going to the hospital. I asked to go with her so I could see Mama. I did not realize when we set off that it would be the last time I would see her alive. When we arrived, Mama was alert with lots of relatives in the room. I did not stay long, but I held her hand and gave her a kiss goodbye before I left with Ellyn after our brief visit. When we got home, Aunt Jane was there, and it seemed as if there was lots of whispering and low voices. I got ready for bed and was in my pajamas downstairs with the relatives when the phone rang just before midnight. Jane was answering the phone in the kitchen, I think, and I went to the hallway in the front of the house and picked up another phone. On the other end was our pastor, Morris House, who told Jane, while I listened, that Mama had passed away a few minutes before he called. He was there with my dad and, I believe, my sister Angela. After crying and not knowing what to do with myself, I was encouraged to go to bed. Our family doctor had left something for me to take to sleep, so after taking the drug, I went to sleep for a few hours. When I awoke several hours later, very early in the morning, I got up and went downstairs to find all of the adults making lists of people to call and things to do. I did not really like the conversation, but I did not want to be alone upstairs. I was numb.

On Saturday, I went with Aunt Ellyn to buy a dress for her to wear, as she had been at the beach prior to coming to Bryan and did not have the proper clothes for a funeral. I remember Chick Sale, the Coca-Cola distributor and family friend, being at our house first thing Saturday with a large cooler with lots of ice and soda water. The visitors started pouring in, bringing food. At the time I did not like pimento cheese, and we were getting lots of pimento cheese sandwiches. A couple of girls a year younger than myself came to visit me, and I was expected to go and chat with them even though it was very awkward for all of us. It was so hard to sit and make small talk with girls from school when my heart was broken and I did not know what was happening or what would happen to me now that my mother was gone. I remember talking with them about all of the food that people were bringing and how nice it was but that I did not like pimento cheese and was afraid that I would be eating it the entire school year, as there were so many pimento cheese sandwiches. Shortly after they left, I was writing what people were bringing in order to write thank-you notes, and I noticed that these girls had brought, you guessed it, pimento cheese sandwiches. Now, not only had I lost my mother, but I had also embarrassed myself. I felt ashamed at the way I had talked about the very gift they had brought.

Later on Saturday, I went to the funeral home to see Mama. She had purchased a beautiful white silk dress on their Holy Land trip in the spring before her death in the summer. It was a beautiful dress, and she had also bought a pearl and jade brooch to wear on the collar of this outfit. Jane was there with us and we knew that something did not look right on my mom. She did not look right to me, as I had not seen a deceased person before and was sad that my mom was not really there. It took a while to figure out, but we finally realized that the dress was on backwards. The funeral director had to take her to the back and redress her, and finally she looked better. Her hairdresser showed up to fix her hair and shared that she had never worked on a corpse before. I could do without that memory. I do not know how long I stayed at the funeral home, but I know that I wanted to run and yet I did not want to leave. Here was my mother, who was about to be closed up in a box. I could not leave her. I could not believe that she had left me.

Many of my mother's friends were at the funeral home. I could hear lots of whispers, many about me, but no one really talked *to* me, they just talked about me. No one talked about death, loss, or dealing with grief. There were so many ideas and feelings, all unspoken!

My brother wrote a tribute to my mom, saying that she would not want us to stop because she died, so I did not stop. I did what I knew she would want me to do, which was to put on a smile and act like nothing had happened; after all, her friends and the rest of the family were acting like nothing had happened. "Oh yeah, Mary died, but time to move on." My brother's tribute was printed and put in a frame, resting in the ridge of the lid of the casket, there for everyone to read. It was a thoughtful gesture, but maybe not such great advice. While I realize that dwelling on a loss is not beneficial, not dealing with it is harmful also. I found out the hard way!

On Sunday before the funeral at our church, we went to the funeral home to tell Mama goodbye. Jane asked me if I wanted to kiss her. I was afraid to even touch her because I was afraid that touching her would create a bad memory. I wanted to stay with her until they closed the casket, but Jane thought that was not such a good idea. So I did not stay. I do remember being outside, alone, in the navy blue suit that I had picked out at the direction of my mother, with the blue-and-white-striped blouse. The sun was shining brightly, there was a hot breeze, the air was very humid, and I could smell my hairspray and feel how sticky my hair was. I felt sick, absolutely nauseated, like I could throw up at any moment. This nauseated feeling became a part of me, my natural state over the next few months. I can still feel the texture of my skirt and the deep sadness. What was I going to do without Mama? Real trauma had set in, and this was just the beginning.

We went directly from the funeral home to the church. I walked into the pew in the first row on the right hand side of the church and feeling like everyone in the audience was feeling sorry for us. I did not like that feeling, but I was feeling awful. I do not remember who I sat next to at first, but I do know that there was a shuffling of seats and I moved next to someone, as I think I was on the end. Morris House, our pastor leading the funeral, said that my mom was a queen. Boy, did he have that right! She was certainly my queen, but why did she leave me and why did she not tell me she was going? I felt angry, sad, betrayed, abandoned, and alone.

After the church service, we formed a motorcade out to the cemetery where she was to be buried in a mausoleum, not in the ground. She was in a sealed box, with a metal cover over it and being placed in a sealed marble tomb in the wall. How would she ever get out "when the trumpet blows" as stated in the Bible?

When the service at the cemetery was complete, we all went home. We had a family meeting in what we called the parlor. Daddy was talking to my sister and brother who were in summer school. He was insisting that they get back to Austin to school, as missing a day in summer school was like missing a week of regular school. So my other support was about to leave. My sister had not been present for me too much as she had two boyfriends hanging out at our house during this whole ordeal, so she had her hands full with not only losing Mama but also with managing her personal relationships. Jane offered to stay a couple of days until Daddy could find a housekeeper. I overheard this conversation and lost it. I did not want a housekeeper; Daddy and I could handle the house alone. I did not want someone to replace my mother. No one could. I had a hysterical fit and ran upstairs to my bed, sobbing. This was just too much! Once my hysteria subsided and I was a little calmer and more reasonable, at least enough to listen, Jane got practical with me. Even though I did not like it, she did make sense. It would be nice to have some help and this person would not be replacing my mother. Mama's friends had found us a new maid who was really good and a self-starter, but my dad wanted someone else to be in charge and it would not be me. He wanted an adult to run the house and to supervise me, to be with me when he was not. Teenager that I was, I did not think I needed supervising and believed I could run the house. I was hoping that my relationship with my dad would become closer, as I did not feel like I knew him very well and I wanted to know him and not be intimidated or afraid of him. He was never loud or the disciplinarian, but he could make you feel very small with just a few words, spoken very softly.

I kept pinching myself during this time, hoping I would wake up from the bad dream. But then I would realize that I was awake and that this was reality. I was miserable. When my brother came home the following weekend, we returned dishes that had been used to bring food to us. He drove and I delivered the items to the doors. There was no discussion about losing our mother, just smiling faces and words of thanks. No one, not even the people that we returned things to, said a word about who was gone. There was this giant black hole that was now a part of our lives that no one talked about.

I wanted to cry all of the time, but I was told not to, and who wants to be around someone who is crying? I was sent off to a summer camp that I had not previously attended as a camper, only as the sibling of a camper, about three weeks after my mother died and reality was really setting in. I remember hearing the new housekeeper complain about my mother's friends not helping to get me ready for camp by sewing nametags in my clothes. The housekeeper was a very nice lady, but she seemed ancient to me. I am sure that she was not, but at thirteen, everyone is old. She had a daughter who lived in Bryan and she, the housekeeper, had grown up in Bryan. One of her granddaughters was in my sister Patty's class and was from a nice family. Mrs. Neely came to live with us soon after my mother's funeral.

I was miserable at camp. Not only was my mother gone, but she also would not be coming to pick me up from camp; she would not be there at the closing ceremonies like she had been for all of my other siblings. Again, I wanted to cry. I was really depressed, and my loss had really hit me. In the early weeks of camp, I had a dream that Mama came to tell my dogs goodbye. It was a very real dream to me and I woke up crying.

My counselor asked me why I was crying and I told her about my dream. She said, "Your mother's okay, right?"

"No, my mother died," I said. I wanted to scream, *Didn't anyone tell you? It seems like something important to know!* Probably no one in my family passed that information along, as everything was fine. Remember, smile and keep going.

I didn't do well at making friends, as I did not really want to talk to anyone. I was alone, something that I would experience most of my life. What thirteen-year-old wants to be different because she doesn't have a mother? What thirteen-year-old wants to talk about their mother and how much they miss her? Most girls my age were fighting with their moms, which is typical, but I was only mad at my mother for leaving me and not telling me that she was going to leave. Trauma is going to a new camp where you do not know anyone and you know that your mom will not be coming to pick you up. It really hit me during camp that it was real: she was not going to come back; it was not a bad dream; it was reality—a horrible reality, but reality nonetheless. The knot of nausea in my stomach was becoming a way of feeling all the time. I was miserable, alone, and saw no way out. There was no way out, only endurance and hoping that someday the pain might not be so great; that maybe someday the stomachache would go away.

My dad and my sister Patty came to the closing of camp to pick me up and take me home, like we had done so many others summers when my siblings had been at camp. I think we were all miserable, missing Mama, but no one said a word. We all just acted like everything was okay. After camp was over, we drove straight home, as my dad needed to work and my sister was missing her boyfriend. I was missing my mom.

I did have something to look forward to when I got home: driver's education. I had passed the written test but I had not done the driving, as I was not yet fourteen and, therefore, not old enough to drive. Everyone else in my school class who was supposed to take driver's ed had already done the driving part. The class was offered through the public school and was taught by the coaches. Since my birthday was in late August, I was the last to drive and the school had already turned in the standard shift car so they wouldn't have to pay to rent two cars when everyone had driven except me. The coaches decided that it was okay for me to go on a drive with one of them. It was legal to drive with an adult at thirteen; you could have a beginner's permit with an adult in the front seat with you. By doing this they could turn in the automatic auto, too, and save the district some money. Besides, they had coaching to do and they wanted to complete the driver's ed class. All of my friends had finished, and they had gone in groups of three, one driving and two observing, and then they would switch. I drove alone with a coach, and we did all of the driving time in two days, driving much of the time through the countryside; thus, the class was complete. I could have a beginner's permit and could drive with an adult.

Even though I was only in the ninth grade, it was my responsibility to drive the maid home every day after school with the housekeeper in the front seat. If the housekeeper did have a driver's license, it was only for ID purposes, as she had not driven in years. Not only did I drive the maid home, but the housekeeper also wanted to stop at the grocery store almost every day. Having to rush home and be responsible was not my idea of fun, but I did it because I was expected to do it.

Besides learning to drive, it was time to get ready for school and my birthday. Two of my friends had a surprise birthday party for me. It was a very special party and I had a great time. It was really nice of them to do that for me that particular year! The surprise party was on Friday night, and on Sunday, my actual birthday, my family had a birthday dinner for me. I remember that Aunt Louise came, which was unusual. One of my gifts was a charm bracelet with charms that Mama had collected at each stop on their spring trip to the Holy Lands; it was a bittersweet gift. I really missed her that night, but no one mentioned her name or that she was missing. There was this huge dark hole in the room, but no one talked about it. I knew that my aunt was there for moral support, but it was not mentioned. An invisible elephant occupied the entire living room!

School started around the first of September and I wanted to try out for the cheerleading squad. I had tried out the last two years, but

I was not selected. Maybe now people would feel sorry for me because I did not have a mother and I would win their vote. There were two cheerleaders selected from each grade. The two girls that had been cheerleaders the last two years were trying out again along with one other person: me. I did not want to try out again and lose, and I felt certain that they would both win again. I was about to drop out when my favorite teacher, Mrs. Todd, the PE teacher, talked me into staying the course and trying out. So I did it and I won! I was so excited!

Being a cheerleader helped me through the school year, but I had trouble sleeping and was depressed. I remember waking up in the middle of the night one school night, and I thought I was paralyzed. I started screaming and my dad came into my room. I did not feel like I could even sit up. My dad talked me down and we finally realized that I had an extremely stiff neck—a terrible crick in my neck, and I could not move it at all. I finally got back to sleep, got up the next morning, somehow got dressed, and drove to my friend's house to get a ride to school. I was hurting, but I did not want to stay home. I wanted to go to school and see my friends. But when we got to school, the pain in my neck was excruciating; I was in so much pain that I had to run to the restroom to throw up. Leaning over the toilet made me see stars, it hurt so bad. I went to the nurse, who called my dad to come and pick me up, which he did, and he immediately took me to the doctor. The doctor saw what bad shape I was in and sent me to physical therapy and to have an ultrasound on my neck. My neck was okay; I just had extremely tight muscles. I still felt nauseated all of the time and started having a headache every afternoon. I was a mess.

The one good thing about being in the ninth grade was being able to go on car dates. I started dating in October and so did my dad, which was certainly odd. My dad was an eligible widower and many of his friends were lining him up with single women they knew, or women were just calling him and asking him out. One divorcee who lived in town was a graduate of UT, like my dad, and owned a huge farm near my dad's property. The housekeeper thought she would be perfect, but my dad did not. Most of the ladies that my dad dated were from out of town and the one that was out of state, who lived in Oklahoma, suddenly had his attention. She was a widow with no children, which my dad seemed to have as a criterion.

I wanted to have a closer relationship with my dad, but it was not happening. As an adult, now I can understand that my dad was really lonely, but so was I, and I became even lonelier as my dad went to Oklahoma almost every weekend. I knew by Thanksgiving that this lady would be my stepmother, five months after my mother died. It was tough to keep smiling and act like everything was fine. My mother would want me to be nice; I did not want to be nice, but I was. I swallowed my tears. I had my birthday without my mom, but the rest of the holidays would be shared with this new female. The most challenging holiday was Easter, when we all went to Daddy's girl friend's hometown. I was miserable, but I kept smiling when I really wanted to cry.

My dad got married a year and a week after my mother died, and I think he would have married sooner, but my new stepmother did not think that would look right. At least we could agree on something. It was really difficult to be present at their wedding even though Daddy was really happy.

I learned to be alone, as I was as a child, but I did not have my mom to rescue and spoil me on occasion to make those times tolerable. My mom was gone, and she left without telling me, which made me angry. So, I went from sad to angry and back again for many months. My dad's generation did not believe in counseling, so there was none of that. There was no one checking on me or asking how I was doing, or if they did, I gave the standard answer: "Fine." I guess everyone thought that now that I had a stepmother, everything was good.

I stuffed my feelings for years, so long that I did not even know that I had unresolved grief issues until I was in college. I recognized them briefly when the movie *Love Story* came out, but I stuffed them right back down. They were too overwhelming to deal with at that time. As I got older and had other relationship issues come up, I realized my loss and began to deal with it. I now recognize how healing it can be to experience and embrace one's feelings. If appropriate, I encourage others to express themselves after a loss, be it a death, breakup, natural disaster, job loss or anything else. Loss is part of life and helps us to appreciate the good, but suppressing my feelings was not good for me, physically or emotionally. Even though I did not recognize my mother's death as a trauma, now that I have put that description to it, neither the event nor my experience has changed; only the word to describe it has.

No loss that I have experienced since my mother's death has been as painful and traumatic, and I doubt any ever will be. As painful as this experience was, I do think that it has given me resilience to withstand life's challenges. I also think that this experience taught me to reach out to people months after a loss. Everyone is there just after the loss, but months later, when you are alone, that is when you need a reminder that people are still thinking of you and sharing your loss.

I still see a reluctance to speak about death. What do we know? What are your beliefs about death? Are you willing to share with others that you are leaving, if indeed you are aware that your time is near? And are you willing to listen to another who wants to talk about death, their own or that of someone else? Maybe if we discussed the mystery of death more often, we would not be afraid of it. I thought with the AIDS epidemic there would be more discussion of both sex and death, but it feels to me as if we have retreated once again to keeping our heads in the sand.

Daddy and Me

My daddy was born in Central Texas on June 15, 1912. He spent his youth between Caldwell and the family farm in the Brazos River Bottom, (the "Bottom"). He and his two brothers had their first educational experiences in a one-room schoolhouse on the farm with a teacher who lived with the family. When the boys got older, the family spent the school year in Caldwell so the boys could attend public school. After graduating from Caldwell High School, where Dadd played the saxophone in the school band, he attended Southwestern University in Georgetown, Texas. His mother had wanted him to attend Washington and Lee, but his father thought that was too uppity for someone from Caldwell. His dad, who had an eighth grade education, was a self-made man, becoming the owner and operator of a large cotton farm that was run like a plantation.

After attending Southwestern for two years, Daddy transferred to the University of Texas, just a few miles down the road from Georgetown, to Austin, Texas, where he received a degree in Business. He was a tow-head (blond) as a child, had black hair as a young man, and hair that had turned white by age 37 when I was born. He had a twinkle in his blue eyes with a nice smile that made people think he was keeping a secret. After graduating from UT, he returned to Caldwell to help run the family farm with his dad and brothers, who had each purchased their own property. He wore cowboy boots and khaki slacks six says a week. While only 5'11", he seemed much larger because he had a huge presence. He met my mother at Crider's, a renowned Texas dancehall near Camp Mystic, while on a double date with one of his brothers. My mother was a counselor at Camp Mystic at the time. They married March 25, 1939. They built a house next door to my grandparents out in the The Bottom but then moved to Bryan in 1948. I heard my dad described as a "pillar of the community," as he served on the Bryan School Board for many years, joined several organizations related to farming and ranching, sat on a couple of bank boards, was a founding member of Briarcrest Country Club, and was an active member of his church, serving on various committees over the years. He was instrumental in the founding of Crestview, a Methodist sponsored home for the elderly. My impression is that he was respected in the community.

When I was a little girl, I was intimidated and somewhat afraid of Daddy, as I called him, as I did not see him very often. When I did, I was usually on my way to bed, or it was Sunday when we were all "proper" and dressed up while sitting at the dining room table having a fancy Sunday lunch. Since my father was a farmer, he left our house in town very early in the morning before the sun was up and did not return until after sunset, at least that was the pattern throughout my childhood. And since I did not see him, I did not know him. We had very little interaction except on the rare occasions when I took a short ride with him to the post office.

Even though I was scared of my daddy, I loved my mama and always wanted to sleep with her, which meant sleeping with him also. In order to keep me from continuously trying to climb in bed with my parents, Daddy agreed to move me from my bed to Mama's bed before he left each day. This worked out to be a good compromise. Daddy and I were both happy.

During the summer, Daddy went with us on summer vacations, but he was never with us for the entire trip, because summer was his busiest time of the year. I do appreciate the fact that he was with us at least some of the time. He did come to Galveston for most of the stay, because I think he liked the gambling casino out on the pier. He also enjoyed our summer trips to Colorado to pick up my siblings from camp, where it was cool and out of the Texas heat.

When our family went to Europe in 1960, Mama, one of my sisters, my brother, and I spent the entire summer traveling. My oldest sister was there with us for the first three-fourths of the trip, and Daddy came and joined us for about three weeks. It was nice for us all to be together, but I will say, having six people traveling together with all their luggage was quite a challenge. No one knew that this would be our last family vacation.

My mother started having severe health challenges in the fall of 1961 when she was diagnosed with breast cancer, had surgery, and began cobalt treatments. I am uncertain of the many issues, as my mother did not talk about her cancer and neither did anyone else. She lost that battle on June 19, 1964. Besides losing his wife, my dad lost the twinkle in his eye.

I longed to have a deeper relationship with my dad. Heck, I wanted to have a deep relationship with almost anyone, as there was a HUGE void in the space that my mother left behind. Daddy and I each grieved alone without talking to each other about the person that we both missed. Daddy remedied his loneliness by dating until he found "the one" with whom he wanted to spend the rest of his days. Some friends introduced them, and the twinkle was back. It was nice to see that twinkle and to know that he was happy.

In February after my mother died, I was chosen as Queen of the Valentine Court, which was mostly a popularity contest at my junior high school. Each grade—seventh, eighth and ninth—voted for a boy and a girl to represent them on the court as Dukes and Duchesses while the King and Queen were chosen from the ninth grade. I had been a Duchess in the eighth grade and had worn a red formal hoop skirt, but the Queen always wore white. I was very flattered and honored to represent my class. Instead of wearing a full white formal, I found a dress with a straighter skirt. I thought that I looked sophisticated and regal, but since the straighter line was a little different, I was not confident in my choice and longed for my mother's guidance. She had been very proud the year before when I had been on the court, but now I faced another big event in my life that I had to navigate alone. Needing validation, I asked one of my best friend's mom's if she thought the dress was appropriate. She approved and I felt good to go.

On Feb 14, 1965, the day that I would be Queen of the Valentine Court in my school, I was feeling pretty good about myself. I was still wishing my mom could be there, but I was pleased that my sister said she would come home from college for the day to attend the presentation that afternoon. I got to leave school early to have my hair done and since I was going for the sophisticated look, my hairdresser and I decided that I should have an "updo". When I left the beauty shop, I thought I looked great. When I arrived home to have lunch with my family, my sister had arrived from Austin and we went directly to the dining room to eat quickly before it was time to leave for the festivities at my school.

Daddy was there at the end of the dining room table, ready to serve our plates. I will never forget the look he gave me as he told me how awful my hair looked. "What were you thinking?" he asked.

I wanted to cry and run away. I picked at my food. There was no time to do anything different with my hair, and at some point, I didn't want to change my hair anyway, just to spite him. I did not get any accolades or "I'm proud of you," which left me feeling sad, ashamed, and alone. I was embarrassing my father. I was the "Queen" of my class but I still couldn't seem to do anything right to get his attention, at least his positive attention. Daddy was a great Critical Parent, and I could hear his mother in his words and voice when he criticized me, relaying that age-old message of "not good enough" that many of us feel. I am sad to say that I do not remember compliments, even though he did say "I love you" on occasion, but did he even like me?

In early 1965, Daddy asked if it was ok with me for him to marry Margaret, the lady he had been dating for several months; she wanted to know. What could I say? I wanted to scream NOOOOOO, but I thought better of it. I knew that I would be leaving home for college in about three years and that it would be unfair for me to tell him I disapproved. So I said it would be fine because I knew it would make him happy.

Daddy and Margaret married in June 1965 at the Methodist church in Guymon, OK, Margaret's hometown. They had the reception at her home and then they left in a private plane on their honeymoon. Our family and friends were left to move many of Margaret's things to Texas. Fortunately, she was NOT bringing much, as I hated her taste for early blond modern compared to my mother's rich, dark English antiques. In negotiating their marriage, Daddy had requested that Margaret move into our house. I am sure it was a challenge to move into another woman's home. It was also much more than what Margaret had, and I think she liked sharing her "good fortune" with her hometown friends, with whom she now seemed to compete about who had the "best". Daddy told her that she could remodel our house when she moved in, which caused huge problems for us, the children. Not that it was our business, but we all sure thought it was. I look back now and see that my older siblings would share their anger with me, get me all stirred up with their issue, and then I would go and "have a word" with Margaret about our displeasure. I was fighting their battles without realizing it, as I lived with Margaret and they did not. I was a mouthy teen, so it worked well for the others, but I was the one who was called a "brat".

Margaret and I tolerated one another, never establishing a close relationship. She wasn't a very nurturing person, but she was thoughtful and very caring of my dad. She promised to look after him until the day he died, as she was five years younger than he. When she became ill with cancer, she was very upset, and her death was quite a struggle, in that she did not want to give up and leave him. She felt like she had broken her contract with my dad. She could not help it, but this was really upsetting to her and she fought death until the end of January 2002.

My relationship with Daddy was strained most of the time because I pushed his buttons. I was not a conformist, and I asked questions about things that he did not want me to know. I challenged him and was not complacent, even though I did my share of standing there and looking pretty. At times I would question the status quo, just to push back, and that was not acceptable. I look back at this tension between us from my pushing back and realize that I was doing it to get attention. If I was good and complacent, I did not get attention, as that behavior was acceptable and expected; asking questions was not, but it did engage him with me at least. I was always looking for his approval. As most young women want from their fathers, I wanted him to SEE me.

My father had a stroke in 2001 while I was in Wichita Falls, Texas, where I was presenting the Dyslexia Intervention Program (DIP) to a group of area teachers, a training program to instruct teachers how to teach students identified as dyslexic. I was notified of the stroke, that it was very mild, and that he would be going to the rehab hospital soon. After he was moved, he was being fed solid food even though he was paralyzed on his left side. This is the story I was told. After a couple of days of eating solid food, my stepmother was feeding him, when he took a couple of bites, sat up, kissed her, fell back on the bed and started turning blue. Margaret hit the emergency response button and called for help, even though he had a Do Not Resuscitate order. The EMT's rushed in and transferred him to the hospital emergency room. He was suffocating and choking on the food lodged in his throat, as he had been unable to swallow. He almost died as a result of eating, and he suffered more damage after that event than from the stroke. Once he was stabilized, he was sent back to the rehab center.

I was visiting Daddy at a rehab center a couple of times when some of his men friends came by. I remember seeing the expressions on their faces when they first saw him. His condition really must have brought home to them their own mortality. They would just stand there for a few minutes, trying to regain their composure. When they did, they didn't know what to say and would only stay a few minutes. I thought my dad looked pretty good, having been through what he had been through, but here was Daddy, who had been a vivacious, powerful man with a huge presence, reduced to sitting in a wheelchair unable to communicate very well. This became a problem for him when he went home because his longtime friends didn't feel comfortable coming to see him. Their wives would take me aside and tell me why they could not visit him, saying it was difficult for his friends to see him this way. I understood. I never shared this information with my dad, and I think he wondered why they stayed away.

When he was released from the rehab hospital, he came home to a hospital bed and round-the-clock care. Margaret hired an agency to provide the services he needed. His physical therapy continued at home, as it was too difficult to transport him anywhere. Margaret was really after him to walk even though he was easily exhausted. Once she passed away in late January, it was determined that he might as well stop his physical therapy. He was resigned to using a wheelchair; he just didn't have it in him to learn to walk again.

As Margaret's health continued to fail, taking care of my dad fell to my oldest sister, Angela, and me, as we both lived in town. I'm not sure how this happened, but in the division of duties, Angela ended up in charge of Daddy's personal care and maintaining the household and yard. I drew the short straw. I got to be in charge of his caregivers and his doctors' appointments, over which we often disagreed. One of his first caregivers, Linda, was really "playing" Daddy. She would schmooze and flatter him *ad nauseum,* and he was falling for it hook, line, and sinker. Those of us observing were disgusted by both of them. I was sad to see my dad falling for this woman's lines, telling him how handsome and young he looked, which was a lie. He looked terrible, like someone who had recently had a stroke. This woman talked her way into being in charge of the other sitters working for the agency and one day announced that her daughter Liz was moving from Arkansas to Bryan to join the agency staff in taking care of him. BIG RED FLAG! After learning of Linda's intention to employ her daughter, I called the agency and asked what their policy was for hiring. They allowed that they did background checks on everyone. I asked if they had done one on Linda's daughter, to which they replied "no", because she was Linda's daughter and she would be ok. I told them that they needed to follow their own policy, do the background check, and get back to me before they allowed Liz to come to my dad's house. After the background check, Liz was not hired. Thus, we dodged that bullet, but there was still Linda. What to do about her was decided by the end of that week.

I did not trust Linda, one of those "intuition" things, and I did not like the way she looked around my parents' home. It did not take long to realize that my instincts were correct. My dad always liked to have some money in his pocket, especially when he went to Sunday School, as he liked to put money in the collection plate, even though he made a monthly donation. His pocket money was kept in his sock drawer, to be available to replace the pocket money as he spent it. One day we realized that some of the money was missing out of the sock drawer. I had my suspicions, but we decided to check the drawer after every shift to see if we could determine who the thief was. And it disappeared when Linda was there. This became a problem for me, knowing how much Daddy liked her and learning that she was stealing from him. We stopped leaving money in the drawer while trying to determine what to do next.

It was during this period that Margaret was hospitalized due to her cancer and one of us stayed with her at all times in the hospital. I was with her on Friday afternoon when my brother, who was in town, called to tell me that he was bringing Daddy up to see Margaret after he dropped Linda at Daddy's house, as her shift was about to end and she needed to do some cleaning before she left. I did not believe her story about the cleaning, so as soon as my brother and dad made it to the hospital, I made a beeline to my parents' house. Linda was surprised to see me and began looking for things to clean. I made it look like I had something to do while I kept an eye on her. When her shift was finally over and she left the house, I was relieved. I sat in the TV room and pondered the situation and how stressful my life had become from looking after my parents. I realized that now, we, the family, were looking after three people, Margaret, Daddy and now Linda to make sure she did not make off with money or valuables.

This is ridiculous! I thought. *How can I relieve the stress? Get rid of Linda.*

I knew that Daddy would be very upset, but I decided that not allowing Linda to work for him would be best for the rest of us. Daddy would just have to get over it. Maybe we could find an honest flirt. I called the agency that afternoon, asked to speak to the owner, told her not to send Linda to work at my father's house any longer, and requested that she find a qualified replacement. When I shared what I had done with my siblings, everyone was relieved and glad that we were back to only two people to look after. I did not tell my dad until Monday morning, just before Linda's shift was about to start. I took responsibility for my actions, but I did not tell him that she had been stealing. He was furious with me and said that she was his best sitter. Fortunately for me, she was replaced by a man, Phil, who could get my dad in and out of the car, which was a challenge due to the paralysis on his left side. He got over his anger at me pretty quickly with his newfound freedom to get out of the house. Phil would even drive him out to the farm to check on things.

There were other times when sitters would call me to say that they had decided to quit in the middle of their shift. The agency sent a new young man, Ken, who was training to be a nurse. Ken really wanted to help the geriatric population, and we thought that he would be a good fit. Daddy did not like Ken, who he talked very ugly to and insulted to the point that Ken called to say he would wait for me to arrive at the house but he quit and I needed to get there quickly. I rushed over and heard my dad spew angry comments at Ken, for which I was embarrassed. I apologized and then Ken left. I was shocked to hear someone I was related to talking to another person the way my dad spoke to Ken. I had never seen that side of him and I certainly did not like it; it was unnerving. I think my dad was uncomfortable having a young male take care of him. Now I was alone, sitting with my parent, who I felt needed reprimanding like a child. How did our roles get reversed? Besides looking after my dad's physical needs, I was now in new territory for me, learning how to parent my parent, which was very unsettling. He was supposed to be in charge, but he was not. Instead, I was, and I did not like it.

Phil, Daddy's favorite sitter because he could help Daddy into the car and drive him places, was diagnosed with liver cancer and could no longer work, so we began the hunt for a replacement. The agency at this time did not have an appropriate sitter so I followed up on a referral to a young lady, Suzie, who was a certified EMT and who was also willing to drive. She negotiated a higher salary than the agency, but she would have more responsibilities and she had more training. I was fine with her salary and when questioned by a male family member who thought it was too much, I asked if he would do the job for that amount. My question was met with silence. Suzie came in the morning, she helped my dad get dressed, she fixed his breakfast, read him the newspaper and then, if he wanted to go somewhere, she took him out in the car. She had the seven to three shift, so she had many duties that required careful attention and a lot of energy. She was up for the job. She really enjoyed it and did an excellent job taking care of him. We appreciated her driving him around wherever he wanted to go and Daddy liked her positive disposition. She was always upbeat with this cranky old man.

One afternoon, both my sister and I went with my dad and Suzie to a doctor's appointment. When anyone would touch my dad, he would bruise. So when the doctor took my dad's shirt off and saw all these bruises, he looked at my sister, me, and then Suzie. "What have you been doing to him?" the doctor asked.

Before any of us could answer, my dad jokingly made some smart comment, but of course the doctor didn't know he was joking. My sister and I were livid. I don't remember exactly what he said, but he was implicating that the sitter had done something, which was not true. My sister and I explained about the bruising, and the doctor relaxed, but Suzie did not. She did not like Daddy's joke at all!

This happened a second time when my dad was at the cancer center receiving a shot for more energy, which he did monthly. Before the shot, there was always blood work, which the doctor would come in to chat about. On this particular day, my sister and I were both unavailable to go to the appointment, so Suzie took him by herself. He was in a room and Suzie needed to excuse herself to go to the restroom. When she returned, my dad was giving the doctor this convoluted story that made it sound like nobody paid any attention to him. The doctor took Suzie aside and asked if my dad was left alone a lot, based on what he had told her while Suzie was out of the room. Suzie was angry because she knew that my dad was never alone. He had 24-hour care, and one of his daughters was there to eat the evening meal with him every night. He was taken out on Saturday night, and then he was taken to Sunday School on Sunday and had a fabulous lunch after that. And she read him the paper daily before taking him to any destination he desired after breakfast!

That did it for Suzie. She felt unappreciated and couldn't believe that my father would be whining and giving the doctors such misleading information. He didn't exactly lie, but he exaggerated to make it sound like he was left alone and nobody took care of him. After they left the cancer center, she took him home and called me to tell me she quit and she would appreciate my coming to his house soon so that she might leave! I was horrified, but I rushed over, as I could tell she was extremely upset. Suzie's feelings were really hurt that Daddy did not appreciate all she did for him. I understood why she might want to quit, but I was having a panic attack wondering how on earth I was going to replace her! Again, here I was with my father, who needed to be reprimanded again. I really did not like being the parent to my parent! It took a while for Suzie's departure to sink in with my father, who did not really understand why she quit. Fortunately, our other regular sitters took extra duty for a few days and finally Suzie realized that she really liked the job, our family and my dad, even if he acted badly at times. She offered to come back to work, but we needed to have some ground rules established in order for her to return. She and I met to discuss how to move forward to make her working conditions more pleasant and to get my dad to behave himself.

Being a former teacher, the only thing I could come up with was a behavior plan like I had used for my students. We decided that a gratitude list was something to try in order to get him in a positive mood. In order for my dad to get to go out in the car, he would have to dictate five things that he was grateful for to Suzie, who would write them down in a notebook. The idea here was: if he had to stop and think about what he was grateful for, maybe he would be more appreciative of her and what she did. And hopefully as a response to being grateful, he would be in a better humor and be kind.

Suzie agreed that it was worth a try and if it didn't work, then she would quit again. But this was the best that we could come up with at the moment. I purchased a notebook and Suzie began to write down the five things my dad was grateful for every day before she put him in the car. It worked, thank goodness! At first he had a hard time thinking of what to be grateful for, but he finally got the hang of it. It was nice to see what Suzie would write and the list grew from one word to two sentences.

Daddy started getting lonely about three in the afternoon, so he would start calling and wanting to know when we were coming over to be with him. It didn't matter if we had something going on, or a meeting, or we needed to be somewhere. He was lonesome and he wanted company. I felt bad that I couldn't be there every afternoon by three o'clock. For the first several months, I put pressure on myself to try to please him, but I was never there soon enough. I finally relaxed, realized that there was no pleasing him, and stopped talking to myself so negatively when I was not doing what he wanted. I could never do what he wanted, as there was always something else for him to complain about

My older sister and I split having dinner with him every evening. One of us would pick up whatever he requested. We didn't cook for him because we didn't want to be insulted about our cooking, but we would gladly take his order and pick up whatever he wanted, and stay to have dinner with him.

Daddy had always enjoyed going out on Saturday night, and even though he was in a wheelchair, he wanted to go to the Country Club, which was right behind his home. There was a ditch between his home and the Club, but we had a piece of heavy metal cut wide enough for the wheelchair to cross the ditch. Granted, it was somewhat bumpy, but it was worth it to him to go out. My husband at the time, Rusty, was very good to my dad. I really appreciated what good care he took of him. He would push my dad in the wheelchair across his backyard very gingerly, avoiding any bumps.

When we arrived at the Club, Daddy would have his usual drink followed by a steak and loaded baked potato. I fixed his baked potato while my husband cut his steak and positioned himself where he could see the door, so he could watch for my dad's friends coming in. Rusty wanted to make sure that Daddy's face was clean and he looked presentable to his friends when they came over to chat.

Besides having dinner with him several times during the week and Saturday night, on Sundays I would bring in lunch after he came home from Sunday School. He wanted the same thing every Sunday from Luby's: chicken with dressing, green beans, mashed potatoes with brown gravy, a roll, and usually a piece of buttermilk chess pie.

There were times when we would have in-depth discussions. One day, he came home from Sunday School and told me that there was no room in heaven. I could see he was terrified. Here's someone in his 90s facing death, not sure when, but knowing he would be there sooner rather than later, and being told that there was no room in heaven. For about a week after that, we had quite the discussions about heaven, and why would you go to a Sunday School when they told you something like that? I didn't believe that that's what God would want someone teaching him. And if God was omniscient and omnipotent, how could it be true that there would be no room for Daddy? Having these conversations with me helped relieve his anxiety. He seemed to appreciate talking about his worries with me better than making idle chit chat. There was a point in our conversation one evening after dinner when he was complaining to me that his grandchildren didn't come to visit him. I pointed out to him that when they did come, many times he was critical. He didn't tell them how glad he was to see them or what he liked about them. Maybe if he started saying something positive to them, they would show up more often. That really puzzled him for a while, but he thought about it and decided that he would try to change. I did hear him speak kindly to one grandchild, so he was working on changing! But then he slipped back to his old ways.

At the time of his stroke and Margaret's passing, I was teaching for the public school district. My dad had a stroke in August, and my youngest daughter was diagnosed with chronic fatigue on the same day that my stepmother was diagnosed with cancer. My oldest daughter had left for college that fall. Fortunately, she adjusted well and staying in Austin was fun for her. Taking care of my dad and stepmother, and trying to look after my daughter while also teaching school was quite a bit for me to handle on an almost daily basis.

At the end of the school year, I realized after my stepmother passed away that my dad would probably only last a year, as he always said he did not want to outlive his second wife because it would be too painful. But here he was, and if I wanted to get to know him, now was my time. I decided that I should resign from my job. Not retire, just resign so that I could go back, hopefully in the next year. I learned that if I continued at the pace that I was keeping during the school year, I was going to end up being the one who was sick.

When my older sister would go out of town for the weekend, I had full responsibility for my dad, which was not really so different, since I already did Saturday night and Sunday lunch, but on several occasions I would hear him whining to the caregiver that he was going to be home alone over the weekend.

I would step up and ask, "What about me? I'm going to be here to look after you, so you will not be alone."

But he didn't buy it. In his mind, he was alone. Hard as I tried, I was still invisible, and I still did not count.

This was made even more evident when my dad purchased an expensive diamond ring for my sister for taking care of him. It really hurt my feelings, especially when two of the four caregivers made sure that I knew, not that they were trying to hurt me, but that he was spending a larger amount of money at a jewelry store accompanied by one of the caregivers. He insisted that his morning caregiver, Phil, take him to the jewelry store to make the purchase. Phil was anxious because he was privy to the amount of money that my dad spent and he was concerned that he would get in trouble for taking my dad to the store. The gift of the ring was difficult for my sister to accept because she knew that I was giving up as much of my own time as she was to care for my dad, and she could see it but he couldn't. He felt safe when she was around, but not when I was, and there was nothing I could do to change it. Lord knows, I tried!

On September 9th, the day before Daddy passed away, he was being kept comfortable, in and out of sleep, but when he awoke that afternoon,

Suzie, the caregiver, asked if he felt like eating something. He decided on some pudding. He was in his hospital bed, turned somewhat on his left side facing the window and looking out into the back yard. My sister Angela and my brother were standing on that side of the room facing him, along with Suzie. I was on the other side of the bed, behind his back where he could not see me. He took a couple bites of the pudding, being served by Suzie, and asked her, "Where is Mary Sue?" To which she replied, "She's here. She's right behind you."

He turned a bit, looked over his shoulder, made eye contact with me and FINALLY saw me. He said, "You're sweet, as sweet as this pudding."

That was what I needed. I could let him go now, and I would no longer be hoping for his approval. I felt I finally had it. I know that that statement probably does not sound like much to anyone else, but it meant the world to me. I could let go. We never had a close relationship, but it did improve and I came to believe that even if we did not agree and that he thought that I was strange, he did love me and respect me.

After coming home from the hospital, where they said that there was nothing more to do for him medically, as he had sepsis and the antibiotics were no longer working, we touched on the subject of his death, me still pushing, but I wanted to know so that I could do my best to carry out his final wishes. I asked him if he thought that this was the end, and he said yes. I asked if he wanted us to be with him or if he wanted to be alone, to which he replied that he did not know. I left it at that; we would see when the time drew nearer.

Daddy's health was failing more with each passing day, and my sister, Patty, who lived in Houston, and my brother, who lived in Dallas, were informed and they came to town. My sister was there the night before he died. The late night sitter failed to give the aspirin as directed during the night so that when Suzie arrived at 7 am he was burning up with fever. She was afraid that he would go into convulsions, so she began holding him. She yelled for Patty in the back bedroom, but got no response, as Patty did not hear her. The telephone in the back bedroom had a different phone number, so Suzie called it, but she still got no answer. We discovered later that the ringer was off. She then called Patty's cell number, but the cell phone was turned off, so she finally called me on the other side of town. Suzie told me what had transpired and asked for help. I called my in-town sister, Angela, and we both headed to Daddy's house. I got there a couple of minutes after Angela did, and as we both entered Daddy's bedroom to help Suzie. Patty came wandering in to see what was going on, having heard nothing until we arrived. It dawned on me that he had made his decision; he wanted us there with him when he left. I was surprised, as this seemed to be happening quickly. Angela went over to help Suzie hold him, his breathing changed, and a couple of minutes later, he was gone, peacefully. There had not been time to call our brother before he slipped away, but he was there soon afterward.

I was glad that I had asked him what he wanted, and I was pleased that it turned out the way it did. Most importantly, I was happy that I was aware of what was transpiring. I was honored to anoint him with oils after he left his body and before the funeral people arrived, a very humbling experience, and I was especially pleased that he had SEEN me.

I felt further validated a little later in the day when I went to look at the gratitude journal in which Suzie had written his daily list of five things he was grateful for. Suzie had him share five things he liked about each of his children, which frightened me at first thought, as maybe there would be nothing below my name, but what he said about me warmed my heart…. Mary Sue: She is always trying to make me a better person. This is the best compliment he ever gave me!

Betrayal and Blessings

Yesterday when I was at the pet store getting some treats for my dogs, there was a family in front of me at the checkout counter: mom, dad, oldest daughter about nine, brother a bit younger at six or seven, and a youngest sister, probably four or five. The dad and older sister were talking with the cashier, the mom was staring into space, the boy was paying attention to the dad and older sister, while the littlest, who was standing right in front of me, was playing with the tags hanging on the end cap. She wasn't bothering anyone and was keeping herself entertained. She was quiet, smiling, and amused as she moved the tags around and flipped through them. Then, her brother saw that she was having fun! The look in his eye was one that I am familiar with. I knew that he was thinking, *She should not be having fun. I want to play with those tags.*

All of a sudden the brother decided to step between his younger sister and the tags to keep her from playing with them; after all, she was having fun and he obviously was not. The little sister tried to push him aside and asked him to move, but he spread out his arms to further block her and would not allow her to touch the tags. She began to fuss and whine, asking him to move when he would not. The dad was still engaged with the cashier, and the mom was still staring off into space. The little girl tried again to touch the tags, and the brother shoved her. She fell to the floor. The mom still did nothing. The little boy stepped toward his younger sister again to block her and show her that he was the boss. She collapsed even further into the floor, now crying as her brother was not only blocking her from her entertainment, but he was being aggressive and mean for no reason.

As I watched this scene play out in front of me, I became upset. I wanted to alert the mom to what was going on, to what she was ignoring, and to tell her that she was allowing a negative pattern to be created. All of these thoughts were based on my own experiences growing up. I previously worked with a Sufi healer who would always see me going into "collapse" when I was faced with a negative situation with a male, be it my dad, brother, or husband. After several healing sessions with him, he asked me why I would go into collapse like that. I thought about it for a nanosecond and remembered my sister-in-law talking about how my brother used to treat me, a story that he must have told her because I certainly did not. I tried to block that memory as it was too painful. I am very empathetic and was in a lot of pain as a child as I felt sorry for everything, even pieces of paper on the highway (this was when people were still throwing trash out their car windows), and paper when it was ripped into pieces or being folded. I especially hated it when one of my friends would hang a Kleenex out the car window and watch it blow in the breeze as we rode down the street until it tore. I was a real mess. So my brother knew how to really upset me, and he enjoyed doing it.

I had a Smokey the Bear stuffed animal that my mom and sisters had ordered for me when Smokey the Bear was doing commercials way back in the early fifties about preventing forest fires, when watching TV was really new. My brother would grab Smokey the Bear out of my arms, hold it over my head by the ear with one hand, and punch the stuffed animal with his other fist, all the while telling me that Smokey was crying and I needed to help him. I would jump up, trying to grab Smokey, but my brother was taller and he would jerk Smokey higher so that I could not reach him. I would be begging him to give my bear back, crying, pleading, and finally falling into a puddle on the floor. Giving up, I would collapse.

I know that my mother was around sometimes and did nothing, just like the mother at the pet store was doing nothing while her son antagonized her little girl. The little boy was such a bully, the mother was oblivious, and the little girl was devastated. I could identify with her, in a puddle on the floor of the pet store crying, feeling completely helpless and not getting any support from an adult and no reprimand for the brother. There were absolutely no consequences for him, and the feelings of the daughter were not validated.

My brother is five years older than I, and my two older sisters are seven and nine years older. I am not sure what happened that caused such discord between my brother and myself, but it began at an early age. I just did not realize it until I was much older. I am still attempting to figure out what happened. When we were really young, we shared a room. My crib was in the room where he slept. I believe that my "hero worship" of him began when he would practice reading to me, which I loved. I still remember his reading *Cochise*. I looked up to my brother, and I thought he was very special; he was my idol. He would check my report card and give me a much stronger chiding than my parents. "How could you not get a check in 'is neat with work,' and your handwriting is terrible!" I do not know why or how my brother took on the authority to reprimand me, but he did, and I continued to idolize him for years! He kept me 'in check," reminding me when I did something wrong.

When our family went on car trips, he was like any other brother, drawing an invisible line on the seat of the car for no one to cross. When we went to Galveston during the summer, I started my begging in the car as we crossed over the bridge onto the island, for him NOT to splash water in my eyes. That salt water burned! But, guess what? On the first trip to the beach the next day he splashed water in my eyes, and he did so every day thereafter. But he was still my hero.

He remained my hero until he got married, and then our relationship changed. Not that it had been a very positive relationship for me, but I still did not realize that until I was in college.

During the summer between my sophomore and junior years in college, I went to summer school and resumed the job that I had had the previous summer, working at a local bank. I had eight- and nine-o'clock classes and then I went directly to work at the bank. My job was to cover for people who were on vacation. Most days, I rushed home after work, took a quick shower, and went out for the evening, only to repeat this schedule the next day. During this particular summer, my parents were on an extended European vacation and asked my brother and sister-in-law to live in the house we grew up in with me to determine if they might like to live there someday. They took the offer and were there to see me come and go; we did not have a lot of time together as I was going to summer school, working at the bank, and going out with friends every night.

I had a friend in college from Houston who had borrowed some money from one of her trust-fund friends to cover an expense that she did not want her parents to know about. Her friend had been very generous and easygoing about the loan, but all of a sudden he was freaking out and demanding she repay him immediately! She did not want to ask her parents, as she had made it this far without involving them, so she contacted me. Since I had a job with a paycheck, she asked me to front some money for her so that he would calm down. I agreed and sent him a check. Letter-writing was still a form of communication back in 1970, so I wrote her a letter during my break at work, informing her of the check and the amount. I took my stationary box in the house after work and left it on the washing machine until picking it up the next morning to take with me to mail the letter. I went out that night, like every other night.

The real recognition of my relationship with my brother came during my junior year in college. My brother called me one spring evening and said that he would be in Austin the next day on business and would I like to have lunch with him? I was thrilled! I felt like I had finally arrived. My brother was taking *me* to lunch, just my brother and me. I was really excited. My roommates couldn't quite understand, but my brother had never done anything like this before, which should have been my first clue. I was living in the sorority house, so the next day when my brother arrived, he came in and called my room. I was walking on air! I rushed down the stairs to meet him, and we walked outside after the usual greetings.

Once outside, I was puzzled to see my stepmother's car parked out front, and she was sitting in the front seat. I was not going to lunch with my brother exclusively, as I had been led to believe, and my heart sank. What on earth was going on? I got in the back seat and asked my stepmother why she was here. She mumbled something, and my brother said we had something to discuss. I was quiet, while my step-mother was making small talk and my brother was driving. He drove us to a nearby park, stopped the car, and then the two of them turned and looked at me in the back seat. I don't remember who asked the first question or even exactly what the questions were, but they did ask me if I did drugs. I was incensed. I did not do drugs, even though some of my high-school friends often offered them to me. I did not want to harm myself and was fearful of what might happen to me, so basically my control issues kept me safe, kind of. I did like to drink, but drugs, no. They kept questioning me for a few minutes and then my brother pulled out a piece of paper and showed it to me and asked me what it was about. It was a copy of the letter that I had written to my friend about sending the check on her behalf. Now, having a copy might not seem like a big deal these days, as lots of people have copiers in their homes, but in 1970, that was not the case. My brother was working at a bank down the street from my parents' house, which I am sure had copiers, so I guess that he had opened my stationary box—remember the one that I'd left on the washing machine?—read the letter I'd writ-ten to my friend, and felt a need to have a copy for future reference. He must have gone to the bank and made a copy, returning the stationary box to the top of the washing machine so that I would be none the wiser.

As I looked at this copy, I was stunned. I could not believe the accusations. My feelings were deeply hurt. If I wanted to do drugs, I could walk a block to the Drag (the street that ran directly beside UT campus) and get street drugs 24/7, a block from the sorority house. I went from crying to hyperventilating. I could not stop and got to that place in crying where you cannot catch your breath. They did not believe me about the drugs or the reason for my covering for my friend. Not only was I hurt by the accusations, but that they did not believe me, which hurt even more. If I was being confronted like this and I did do drugs, I would have said so, but I did not do drugs; alcohol was quite enough to keep me entertained! I must admit, I did drink too much, but that was not what they were asking, and I did not realize at the time that alcohol is a drug. When I did not admit to something that I did not do, they finally decided that it was time to go to lunch. I asked to go home, but they would not let me. They insisted that I come into the restaurant, so I went in and sat there at the table with them and sobbed. I did not care if people were staring at me; that was nothing compared to the pain I was feeling. Not only was I disappointed that my brother did not come to take me to lunch like I thought he was, but he had also been holding evidence against me for at least six months. He never asked me about the letter, as I thought brothers were supposed to do; he just presented it with my stepmother, and I am sure they had discussed it. I still didn't realize how much he didn't like me, and it would take many more years and several more incidents before I did.

After they finished eating—I did not eat, as I had no appetite and was still crying—they returned me to the sorority house. We pulled up in front and my stepmother asked if I wanted her to tell my dad, which set me off even more! I yelled at her that there was nothing to tell except that the two of them had come to Austin and accused me of doing drugs, which I did not do! I got out of the car and went in the house. My girlfriends were waiting for my report of my lunch with my brother. I walked in and they were astonished at the appearance of my red, tear-stained face and swollen eyes. I was so exhausted from crying that I could barely tell them what happened. When I did, they were shocked. They knew me, they lived with me, and they knew that I did not do drugs. I was wounded, hurt, and felt betrayed. This man, this brother, was acting like he was out to get me. I could not see this at the time, and I certainly did not know where I fit in the family.

I did tell my dad the next Friday when I went home. I went to his office on the way into town. I told him about my visitors and their accusations. I told him I did not do drugs, but I did smoke, and now I was going to smoke in front of them. He did not say much; he just listened. I am sure he had been forewarned, but he did not scold me or talk badly about them.

The years went by, and my brother would make comments about me and my life, but nothing like this betrayal ever happened again. When I was divorced and living in Houston with my two young daughters, I was having a conversation with both of my parents (Daddy and Margaret, who I now consider a parent) one evening; they were each on a phone at their home in Bryan. I do not even remember what we were discussing, but my brother Thomas's name was mentioned in reference to the topic along with his negative comment about me. I suddenly heard my own voice say, "Thomas is always trying to make me look bad." There was silence, mine included. It was like an arrow had flown through the air to hit a bullseye, its target. It was a profound truth. Nothing I had consciously thought about, but here it was. This was exactly what had been going on all of my life. None of us realized it until those words came out of my mouth. I was thinking, *Who said that?* and then I realized that I had said it. We were all surprised, but it felt so "right" that none of us really said much after that. I think we just got off the phone.

After this phone call, my relationship with my brother changed again. I realized that my brother did not like me and that I needed to give up my expectations of having a "brotherly" relationship with him. I recognize that we do not get to pick our relatives and that it is possible to not like a family member, but I also realize that you can learn to be a "good sister or brother." We did not get those instructions I am sad to say. We did not receive the same script on "how to be a member of a family," of different people with different perspectives.

Fortunately for me, I learned early that "family" can mean many different things and that no family is the same, even though there are many common threads. A family can be a group of people who are blood relatives and a family can be a group of friends who love, support, and hold you accountable, who really KNOW you and accept you as you are. I found dear friends, male and female, brothers and sisters, to become my family, and we are blessed to face life's challenges and accomplishments together, as a family would. I am blessed and grateful to have a wonderful family of friends.

Do you have a challenging situation with a sibling? If so, what have you learned from this relationship? What have you learned about yourself?

Failing to Get My "MRS" Degree

I went off to college in the fall of 1968 from the small conservative town of Bryan to Austin, Texas, to a liberal college in a liberal city. I had a difficult time adjusting to college. I had lived in a large house with fourteen-foot ceilings before moving in to a small dorm room in which the bed pulled out of the wall and the closet was about thirty inches wide. And this small space I shared with a roommate. There were very good things about it, as everything was easy to reach; and there were very challenging things about it, namely, claustrophobia.

My roommate had lived in Bryan when we were young. She went through first and second grade with me and then she moved to Waco, Texas. We found out that we were each going to UT and decided to be roommates our freshman and sophomore years of college. We both went through Rush in the fall of 1968. The Greek system was beginning to die and was not as popular as it had been, but it was something we both wanted to do. All the women in my family had been in sororities, and most of them belonged to an organization called Pi Beta Phi.

I was expected to go through Rush, which I did. It was quite fun, intimidating, and scary all at the same time. Being from Bryan, I didn't know much about Rush, how it worked, or what happened in order to get a group of girls to be in your sorority. The city girls were very aware of the process and how it worked. The rushees, as those of us going through Rush were called, were grouped alphabetically to go to parties at each sorority house. We would stand outside each house until we were invited inside to the party. While waiting outside, the rushees shared horror stories of girls being cut, which meant being eliminated from the invitee list of a sorority and therefore no longer being considered for membership in that sorority. The first round of parties was the time that most girls who were legacies (had a family member of said sorority) were cut. Supposedly, if you made it past the first round of a legacy sorority, it meant that you had a place in that group if you wanted it. The same was true with a rushee. If she cut a sorority, she was indicating that she did not want to be a part of that group.

I heard that the sorority that I was a legacy to cut a bunch of other girls who had been legacies to the sorority too, and their feelings were hurt. I didn't like that about Rush, people getting their feelings hurt. I went on and I went to another sorority the last night and seriously considered pledging it, rebel that I am, because they were so nice to me and seemed so excited to have me. The Pi Phi House, where I was a legacy, seemed excited, but not like the other house that I went to. I learned later that "stealing" a rushee from another sorority is a big coup. My roommate was going to the other house that I had been to that night, so I was somewhat torn, but at the last minute I decided that I would pledge my family sorority because I knew that I had a place, since all these other people had been cut.

I found sorority life interesting. During Rush, everyone was very excited to see me and they gushed over me, but as soon as Rush was over, I was just another girl. This abrupt switch took some getting accustomed to. The day we pledged we got our bids, which means you find out what sorority invited you to join them that you had picked that you wanted to join. After receiving your invitation, you went to the house to be met by active members of the sorority, and they were excited to see you. The sorority I pledged assigned you to a mentor, a buddy, to look out for you and to help you get started in every aspect of college life, including the sorority. One of the girls from Bryan, a couple years older than I was, who was in the sorority, became my Beta bud. She gave me a pledge pin, which was the point of an arrow, with the complete arrow being the sorority symbol. The Beta bud is a temporary mentor until you have what's called a Big Sister, who is your permanent mentor. The first meeting we went to, we wore our Beta bud pins and were given instructions about how to behave when we were on campus, how to behave at parties, and what the rules and regulations were. You weren't supposed to walk across the dance floor with a drink or a cigarette in your hand. Very important and certainly unladylike. When you went to class you were always supposed to wear a dress or a skirt, no jeans or slacks, and you were to wear your pledge pin, the Beta bud pin.

I thought it was really interesting how we were getting instructions as to what to wear and that we needed to wear our pins. I did it because that was what they told me to do, until the next week.

When we went to our next weekly meeting, we were told not to wear our Beta bud pins and that if we wanted to wear jeans to class, we could, and we probably should because the attitude on campus toward Greeks in the late '60s was not very friendly. You have to remember, this was during the Vietnam War. The student body was very tense, young men worried about the draft, and then there were the hippies and lots of druggies. There was a lot of anger and uncertainty. There were demonstrations taking place on campus and on the Drag, the street just across from campus and one block from our sorority house. Those in the Greek system decided it was best to try to blend in with the rest of the students instead of standing out as a member of a Greek organization, which represented white privilege. The Greek organizations were thought of as elitist, and I would say they probably were.

While it was interesting being told what to do by your peers, like I said, I was from a small town, and I didn't really understand sororities or how they worked. I didn't understand exactly what it meant to be a member except everyone in my family had been in a sorority and now I did have a group of instant friends. It was nice to have people to hang out with and go places with and we usually had similar interests because we came from similar backgrounds. The flip side was meeting girls who had been cut by my sorority, legacies in particular, who, once they found out what sorority I was in, did not want to have anything to do with me. That was painful, as I was not the one who cut them yet they would not give me the time of day.

We had required pledge meetings every Monday night, and study hall most other nights. These were things that you had to do in order to be initiated into the sorority. You also had to take a test, know who all the founders were, know the password and handshake, introduce yourself and be able to identify every active member, and you had to have a 2.0 grade point average. I don't know if most people realize that most sororities, including mine, were formed from Bible study groups. My sorority was the first sorority ever established, and it was at Monmouth College in Monmouth, Illinois. Years later, several founders were suffragettes, helping women get the right to vote. One member was the founder of what became the League of Women Voters. Pi Beta Phi was also the first sorority established at the University of Texas at Austin.

I immediately started worrying about whether or not I was going to make my grades. I was overwhelmed with reading, as I was taking geology, psychology, sociology, and philosophy, all these –ologies. In 1968 you had to have an advisor sign off on your required courses. You registered for class by standing in line for each class in Gregory Gym along with many other Freshmen. When you finally got to the front of the line, the class might be full and then you would have to go back to your advisor's office to find another class to register for, hoping that it would still have space. I had to jump through these hoops a couple of times to end up with the classes that would count toward my degree but were not ideal to be taking all at once. It was very difficult to keep up and, instead of comprehending what I was reading, I would find myself thinking, "What if I don't make my grades?" Well, I'll tell you right now, I didn't make my grades the first semester, but I did make them the second.

The evening after we received our invitations, each sorority had what was called "pledge line." Talk about sexism! The fraternities would tour the different sorority houses to see the girls the sororities had pledged. In our particular case, they had us all line up upstairs. The fraternity boys came over, some of them, and our pledge class had to walk down the steps. We were on parade, which really rubbed me the wrong way.

After a few weeks, when we all arrived for our Monday-night pledge meeting, we got in trouble because we weren't wearing our pledge pins, so we were all sent back to our rooms to get them. This was kind of the icing on the cake for me. There were always conflicting messages. At least, that was the way I felt. I didn't quite understand why all the girls from the big cities went along with these demands and these changes. I just didn't get it. Anyway, I had to go back to my dorm to get my pledge pin and then go back to the meeting. By the time I got back to the sorority house, I was furious. Everyone else had returned and was downstairs in the basement, while I was considering turning my pin in and de-pledging.

As I was going downstairs, I made the statement that I thought I was just going to turn my pin in, that I was tired of this ridiculousness, when I was grabbed by a couple of upperclassmen, one being my Beta bud, my friend from Bryan, who took me aside. Basically, they kept me from going downstairs and turning in my pin because they held me up until the meeting was over. They wanted to know why I felt the way I did, so I tried to explain.

The sorority would tell us things to do that, to me, seemed ridiculous, like spending meeting time going back to get my pin across the campus. I just didn't agree with all the things that were going on. I did enjoy the other pledges, getting to know them, and spending time with them; that was fun.

We had what were called match dates, where every weekend in the fall, our social chairman would match up our pledges with a group of fraternity pledges. One weekend, our pledge trainer, who was from my hometown, was excited that her boyfriend, who was the social chairman of his fraternity, matched me with his little brother, his assigned mentee. The pledge trainer was excited, so I was excited. This was back in the days before cell phones, so when your date called you to come pick you up, you would describe what you had on and meet in the lobby where he would come and find you. This fella was from Amarillo and supposedly the star pledge. He called my room, I told him what I had on, and I went out into the lobby of my dorm, Kinsolving.

Out in the lobby, I stood with all of the other girls waiting for their dates to appear. I looked around. I waited probably fifteen or twenty minutes and no one ever came up to me. I don't know if he even told me what he had on. Anyway, I finally gave up, went back to my room, and was really puzzled and disappointed. I wanted to call my pledge trainer to tell her, but I knew I couldn't reach her as she would already be at the party with her social chairman boyfriend. I realized that I had been stood up and my feelings were really hurt. He obviously did not like the way I looked, so he left. I decided to go to the cafeteria and get something to eat, thinking food would make me feel better. My wing of the dorm was getting really quiet and I was feeling lonely, as everyone else was going out. Everyone I knew had a date.

The cafeteria was about to close and since I wasn't going anywhere else for dinner I went to the cafeteria. There weren't many people there, but I spotted one of my pledge sisters, who was from Amarillo, where my match date was from. I didn't tell her anything about what was going on with me, but she started talking and made the statement that she was coming in to grab something quick to eat because she was going to go meet the fellow who I had been assigned to as a match date. She was going to the match party with him because his date didn't work out. She had no idea what had really happened and I did not tell her.

I knew that I didn't look great, but I didn't look that bad. After hearing what this pledge sister was telling me, I felt even worse. I'd *never* had anything like that happen to me. I had always had dates. I had always been popular in high school, and having a date was never a problem. I was devastated. I don't know what I did, except go back to my dorm room and feel miserable. To make matters worse, I think it was a football game weekend when my parents came to town and I had to admit to them what had happened. I was ashamed and terribly sad, and I lost what little confidence I had. But I will share that karma works. Years later, when I was a twenty-eight-year-old divorcee, my roommate and I went to a club one night and met these two men who came back to our apartment with us. Something about one of them seemed familiar, maybe because we had all gone to the same university.

After a few drinks, one fellow slipped and called the other, the familiar one, by a nickname, the same nickname as the guy who stood me up during my freshman year. I let it go for a few minutes, no comment, but my roomy and I realized that these two guys were married and had lied to us. She and I were furious, but we let them continue on for a few more minutes until they started hitting on us, and at this point I let them both have a piece of my mind for lying to us. Then I turned to the guy who stood me up and threatened to call his wife. He deserved to be caught and I knew if I wanted, I would be able to find her. I told him I now realized that he'd done me a favor by standing me up, as he was not worth my time because he was a sleazy cheat, a dishonorable man. I let him think that I was going to call his wife, and I hope he squirmed for many months, but I did not waste any more time looking for his wife.

Back to sorority life. The next big thing that happened with my pledge class was what was called the pledge prank. Again, this was in the fall, shortly after we had pledged. It was in October because it was during Oktoberfest, which was a big celebration in New Braunfels, a small German community near Austin that a lot of people went to on the weekend. On this particular weekend in October of 1968, the University of Texas was playing SMU in a football game, and I had a date with my family friend from SMU.

We were told that we needed to play a prank on the actives. After we heard about all the things that previous pledge classes had done, and how this was something that pledges always did in the fall, we were expected to come up with an elaborate plan. We had groups of people who made all these plans about the things that we would do, and we came up with the idea that we would do our pledge prank at halftime of the football game, which was also parents' weekend. There were cars of pledge sisters who did not go to the football game, but came and picked up those of us who did at halftime, drove us over to the sorority house to do our pledge prank, and brought us back to the stadium before halftime was over. I don't remember exactly how many girls lived in the house, but there were three pledges for each bedroom.

Since my last name started with a "P," I was with two other "Ps." We had a sack with our names on it, and it had a list of things that we were to do on the sack—things we were to put in the sack. The directions were all there. Somehow we were not instructed as to what to do with the sack at the end and our sack got left in the room where we did the prank. I will say our pledge prank was great. One of the things I still remember that I thought was the most fun, or the most fun to watch the results of, was all the millions of Pappagallo flats that were thrown into the foyer. Since it was parents' weekend there were a lot of parents going in and out of the house. Pappagallo shoes were very popular, especially the navy blue ones, and since you all had to look alike, everyone had at least one pair; some girls had two or three pairs.

We took all the Pappagallo shoes out of every closet in the house and threw them in the foyer. Can you imagine how many size sevens there were? Those particular shoes, they kind of started fitting your feet and the actives complained that they never actually found their own shoes. But when you saw the parents walk in the house and see all the shoes in the middle of the floor, it was hysterical. We did a great pledge prank, at least we thought so, and we thought that the actives would think so too. After all, this was what we were supposed to do. The parents thought it was good and clever that we had left the game to pull the prank. Some of the actives were impressed, but some were really angry. They were so angry that they put out an all-points bulletin that we were to be in the basement at the sorority house the next morning at seven a.m.

Now, I wasn't in my room, and I didn't want to answer my phone. I was with my parents. I had gone incognito to stay with them so I wouldn't get called out for the pledge prank. I kept acting like I didn't know until my other "P" friend really put the pressure on me to come. Most of us showed up. I won't say all of us. There were some people who, even though they knew it was happening, chose not to come, but they didn't really get in trouble for it.

Those of us that went to the meeting got chewed out for our pledge prank, which, again, I thought was very confusing. This was something we were told was expected of us. Every pledge class for eons had done pranks, and we had to do it, and we needed to do a really good job, which we did. Again, I was a small-town girl really questioning how incongruent all this was. The girls from the big city "knew about sororities, knew how it was," and they just all took it. I don't know what was wrong with me, but I didn't like that about the sorority. Even so, I really did enjoy my pledge class friends. Since I did not make my grades, I didn't get initiated the first semester when they all did, and instead got initiated in the fall right before Rush.

We all moved into the sorority house as juniors and loved living there. It was really fun, a continuous slumber party, and our friendships became even deeper. During the summer, we all moved into an apartment together for summer school. At some point late in our junior year, some of the girls were talking about staying in an apartment our senior year. I pointed out to them that they were crazy because living in the house was a no-brainer; we were very spoiled there. We lived a block from campus, we could go downstairs in the morning and place our order for breakfast, and the breakfast cooks would fix us anything we wanted. We had a nice buffet lunch that was offered for several hours so we could go to class and get back in time to eat, and then we had a sit-down dinner every night, with waiters who served us, picked up our plates, and took them back to the kitchen so we never had to do any grocery shopping, cooking, or cleanup. We just walked downstairs to eat and got up and left after dinner. The best part of being in a sorority was living in the sorority house. I wish I could move back in!

I told my friends that if they wanted to live in an apartment and take care of themselves, that was fine, but I was going to stay in the sorority house because I knew that was going to be the end of that sort of treatment for myself until I moved to a nursing home at an old age when my body no longer worked. Anyway, I did really enjoy my friends a lot and still do; to this day I spend time with a group of them every year.

The only negative thing about living in the sorority house during this time became walking to campus, which meant crossing the street called the Drag. The Drag is the main street that runs beside the university where, during the early seventies, there were lots of demonstrations, hippies, druggies, political activities, and homeless people, many of whom were panhandlers, a term used for those asking for money. There was a lot of drug-dealing happening on the Drag. Some days, getting through the crowd and being harassed were almost more than I could stand. It made me not want to go to class. Those of us who lived in the house tried to look as much like the "drag rats" as possible to avoid being noticed. Then, after we crossed the street to get onto the campus, there were a lot of different organizations lined up along the walkways going to our classes. There was an organization raising funds for a free breakfast program for kids. This was the result of one of the free civil rights groups offering free breakfast to children in Austin, which I think was great, and this particular group was the precursor to what are now the free breakfasts offered in public schools, but I didn't like being hassled every day for money, which I was. The girls who lived in the sorority house quit taking their wallets or purses to class; we only took a notebook and a pen. I remember one day being stopped and asked to donate, and I said I didn't have any money. So the person said, "Well, how about those pearl earrings you have on?" They weren't real pearls, they were fake, but he thought since I looked like a sorority girl, even though I was trying to be incognito in my jeans and shirt, he would ask me to donate my earrings. I told him that they were fake. Things like that made me uncomfortable. There were always people confronting each other, hippies and vets and demonstrations for the war, demonstrations against the war. It was a very tense time and, unfortunately, I could not get to class without walking through all of the chaos.

One day I was walking behind a young man who was asked by a panhandler if he had any spare change, and in response, the young guy put his hand in his pocket and pulled out his change. He looked through the change and then said, "No, none to spare," put his change back in his pocket and kept walking. I had to smile but was nervous that he was going to be attacked. Sometimes there would be things happening on the Drag and police would come and use tear gas, which was not pleasant; being so close to the Drag, we suffered some of the effects of it. A couple of times, people would start running and they would run into our house. The front door of our house was not locked at the beginning of our junior year, but that was soon remedied. A very valuable painting given to the sorority by one of our alumni was stolen off the wall during one of those incidents.

We spent many hours in meetings talking about what to do about the front-door situation. A committee decided we would all be given plastic key cards to get in, and if you lost your key card, you would have to pay for everybody else to get a new one. The first weekend after our key card distribution, the person who had instigated the whole idea of the cards was the one who lost her card, but she did not have to pay for everybody's new cards. We went to a keypad instead, which seemed to be a better solution.

In 1970, the year before moving into the sorority house, I was living in a private dorm that was about four blocks from campus. This was during the Kent State shootings. After hearing about Kent State on the news, my parents immediately called me and told me to stay off campus. This inspired me to immediately go to campus because there was a sit-in demonstration on the mall at UT. None of my good friends went with me, but I joined a sorority sister a couple of years older whose parents were good friends of my mom while growing up in Fort Worth. Her name was Sarah and she was from Galveston, so we would see her family a lot when we were in Galveston. We stayed on the mall until well after her curfew. Since I lived in a private dorm without a curfew, she came with me back to my dorm to sleep. We bonded over demonstrating!

Most of my other sorority friends were never politically active. Not that I was that politically active, but I did feel like we needed to take a stand. Even within my sorority, I was probably more liberal than most, even though I had come from a conservative small town. Immediately when I got to Austin, Texas, I heard about the fortune teller, Madam Hipple. I made an appointment to see her as quickly as possible. I kept the notes that she gave me, and when I think back about them, she was right, but she could have given this message to any number of college kids. Anyway, once I was let loose, I started thinking for myself a little more. What a novel idea, or maybe I'd always thought for myself but I hadn't been able to act on it; that was probably more the case. Was I to conform or be a trendsetter and maybe cause people to think differently? I was always pushing the envelope.

I found that I was very interested in mysterious things that were not the norm. I was introduced to a program called Silva Mind Control. The name gave it bad press, as those who did not know what the classes were about thought that you were learning to control other people's minds, but that was not the case. I heard about this class my freshman year and took the first class offered in Austin, learning many techniques that I still use today. My favorite is programming my mind to wake me up at a certain time. It has never failed me! This was my first step out of the box that I had been raised in, and I loved learning this information.

I went to this class alone, as my college friends were not interested in learning these "weird" things; staying in the conformist's box was safer. This program is still around and is now called the Silva Method. I have had a refresher, and it is still very powerful and easy to use.

My junior year, I needed one more history credit and the mainstream classes were full so I got into a contemporary class. This class was taught in a new auditorium with lots of lights, bells and whistles by a very progressive teacher. The subject matter of this class was about issues that we were facing a the time. I don't remember the exact name of the class, but I do remember that we were to write a paper at the end of the semester starting with a revolution and then creating a whole new society. Well, little ole me had a really hard time with that concept. I was in support of change, but I did not know how to do it. I needed more exposure and hoped that I would learn something in order to write my final paper.

During one class, the professor brought up racial relations and one of the students publicly convinced him to allow the African-American students in the class to make a presentation, so they did.

The other students, all the rest that were not African American, were in this class because we were curious and wanted change. I do not know what happened, but the presentation did not go well. The African-American students were all up on stage, and someone in the audience asked what we could do to help and what we could do to change, which really set a couple of them off. The presenting students came running off the stage, down the aisles, yelling at those of us in the audience. I remember one girl looking at me and telling me how she always had to play with white baby dolls. I regretted she had to play with those baby dolls, but I wasn't the one in charge of making the baby dolls. We were asking what we could do to change things. This was good to know. I mean, writing the manufacturers of baby dolls would be a step in the right direction, but the discussion became very hostile, very heated, and very uncomfortable. I couldn't wait for class to be over and to walk out the back door. I wanted to slip out the closest door at the moment but certainly did not want to be seen! It was the anger from students who had been allowed the class time to talk about issues we thought should be talked about, but it ended up getting out of hand.

As the semester was about to end, I needed that final paper, but I could not figure out what to write. I chatted with my friends about it and no one could help me except one friend who wrote a story, which was ridiculous, like out of a juicy novel, and so I didn't turn it in. Finally, the boy who I was dating told me he would be glad to write the paper for me if I would type all of his papers for him. I was a very proficient typist, so I typed lots of papers for many people, especially when I needed some extra money. I started typing his papers and he began writing mine. I read the paper that he wrote for me and thought it was certainly better than what I could come up with, and certainly better than the juicy piece my Pi Phi friend wrote. The boyfriend's paper sounded more legitimate, so I typed it up, turned it in, and went home for the summer.

My grades came around the end of June and I had a "Q" in that particular contemporary history class. I called my teaching assistant to ask why. He asked me to come in and talk with him so I had to drive to Austin. I arrived at his office, we sat down, and he began sharing with me that as he was grading my paper, thinking it was a very interesting paper, he had the television on watching, I believe, C-SPAN. He was watching a rerun and my paper was the speaker's talk. I don't even remember who the speaker was, but I absolutely could not believe it. The TA was upset with me because I had plagiarized, and that was why he wanted me to come in in person. I was so angry and so upset, I immediately blurted out what had happened. I couldn't believe that my boyfriend had done that to me. What a rat! The teaching assistant said he probably would have never caught me if he hadn't had this TV program on, but my paper was this person's speech verbatim. I was livid and very embarrassed, but since he saw my reaction, he believed me. He was glad that I had not been the one who plagiarized.

He said, "I'll give you a Q, so you can make it up, and you have till the end of next semester to turn in a different paper that you have written yourself." He gave me some pointers and some guidelines about how to do it, and he forgave me for asking someone else to write my paper.

I just told him, "You know, it's beyond my capability to think that way and write about it." And I think that he understood. I thought it was very nice that he gave me another chance and didn't fail me, and I did finally get a paper together. It was one of those things that you only hear about happening on college campuses. Such is life. Sometimes the lessons that you learn outside of class are more important than what you can learn in class, and since I didn't spend a lot of time in class, most of my learning was done out of the classroom. Life experience was the best teacher in this case. I was learning to take responsibility for my life and my actions or inactions. I was learning to rely on myself, not others, and to figure out what I needed to do in any given situation. I was learning that responsibility is a moral obligation to behave correctly, for ME to do the right thing, to do my own work no matter the challenge.

Even though I was a junior, I still did not feel like I was part of the group. There was a drinking club where the popular girls would pick other popular girls to join this club, which I really wanted to be a part of. I decided maybe if I started drinking more, maybe I would be asked to participate in this club. I wasn't picked the first semester of my junior year, but I was finally picked the next semester, which added to lots of problems for me from drinking too much. This drinking club was called Bored Mortars, the opposite of the Mortar Board, which is an academic honor society. The drinking club was made up of girls from six different sororities. They met once a month on a Thursday night at a beer garden down near the Capitol. It was always lots of fun, with tons of people. It was nice because it was outside in the back of this establishment. There were interesting people besides the college kids; city folks and legislators showed up when they were in session. Years later, when I joined a 12 Step group, I learned that one of the group members had been the founder of this drinking club, and there were lots of other former members of Bored Mortars sitting around me at this meeting. The best thing about Bored Mortars is that it led many of us to the 12 steps of Alcoholics Anonymous and learning to take responsibility for our lives. I had lots of support from these wise women.

I didn't like attending weekly sorority meetings on Monday nights because it seemed like we got into arguments over the silliest things. We could spend hours arguing over whether or not we were going to have hot dogs, hamburgers, or chicken at our Spring Fling. For the last couple of semesters of my college career, I arranged to have classes on Monday nights so I would not have to attend chapter meetings. The last semester, I was out of options for Monday night class. Just after I arrived at my first meeting in years, my good friend reintroduced me to the chapter, stating that I had done my best to avoid meetings and that people probably didn't know me or who I was because I hadn't been at a meeting in a couple of years. That was true, but embarrassing.

Being at the University of Texas from 1968 to 1972 was a very intense time. The military still had the draft. There were lots of protests, lots of unrest, and high anxiety. Most of my sisters and their friends had all graduated from college and most got married immediately. There were only a couple out of our group, about six to eight, that hung out together regularly, that were getting married, so things were changing. I know that I was surprised to be forced to look for a job. That had not been my plan. I don't believe it had been the plan of several of my friends, either. Granted, they might have wanted to work, but I think we all thought that we'd find a husband and get our MRS degree. In the end, that wasn't the case.

Things had calmed down some by the spring of 1972. They weren't quite as intense, but still, it was somewhat of a relief to leave Austin, get a job, and live in another city. Time to do something different. We were growing up and needed to put our college experience behind us and to good use. Several of my sorority sisters moved to Houston. We were, if not roommates, living close to one another. We all hung out together. Some of our guy friends that had been in law school graduated and moved to Houston also, so that was nice. They weren't boyfriends, but they were boys that were friends that we could call and ask to take us to different events, as back then you needed a date.

When I reflect on my college days, I remember the fun we had and the lifelong friends I made, but the unrest that was felt during that time was unnerving, even if I did not realize it at the time. Today, we are once again dealing with the same issues: civil rights, women's rights, and drug abuse. Hopefully we'll do a better job of addressing these issues since we haven't resolved them yet.

My Friend Who Died of AIDS

November 24, 1988. In the second semester of my sophomore year of high school, while I was still learning the ropes, I took Typing II so that I might be proficient in typing, as I knew that it would serve me well, which it did. I became a fast typist and typed lots of papers not only for myself but also for college friends for extra money. I really enjoyed typing, and I still do. The problem with taking this class was that it put me in a weird lunch group, not with any of my girlfriends. I did have an older guy friend whose name was Jeff. He had the same lunch period without any of his friends, too, so the two of us ate lunch together almost every day for the semester. We ate so much greasy Mexican food that his hair started getting greasy and my face began to break out! Since he was two years older, he went off to college at the end of that school year while I had two more years of high school. I would see him when he was home during breaks, and then we really renewed our friendship while I was an undergrad at the University of Texas and he was in UT law school. He was the kind of guy who was a really good friend, the kind that you could talk with and share innermost thoughts that you would not share with a boyfriend. He was always there when I needed a shoulder to cry on, and if I needed an escort and was not dating anyone or they were not appropriate for the event. Jeff was not only my "date when you need a date" but he became good friends with several of my girlfriends and was an escort for them also. Upon our graduation from UT the same year, we all moved to Houston—me to teach, one gal to work as an accountant, and another who became a pharmacist, while Jeff went to work for the city of Houston as a city attorney. Our role as "date" continued after moving, and we all hung out and partied together. This went on for a couple of years until we all began having lives that still included the core group but were getting diluted with new friends and new living arrangements. One of our girlfriends, who stayed at UT and got her masters in accounting, became a CPA. Then, after moving to Houston for work and to join the gang, she enrolled in law school. She was a smart cookie and had many other talents! After she got her law degree, she and Jeff decided to open a law firm. They asked one of her classmates from U of H law school to join them, and he did. Ironically, he was from our hometown but was unknown to Jeff. I knew who he was, as he was the younger brother of a fellow that I had loved to flirt with who was in the class behind me when I was in high school. I could easily make the older brother uncomfortable, as he was really shy. These three formed their law practice, but our college group rarely socialized anymore.

In January of 1988, while I was reading Shirley MacLaine's book, *Out on a Limb*, I got this hit that Jeff, my long-time friend, was sick. I felt compelled to talk with him. I asked him to go to lunch and while we were eating, I told him that I had received a message that he was sick. I wanted him to know that if there was anything I could do to help him, I would. He was startled at first at my "knowing" but he looked relieved and shared that he had the first stages of HIV, human immunodeficiency virus, the precursor to AIDS.

The AIDS epidemic was in full swing and gay men in Houston were being diagnosed and quickly dying, as there was no cure. It was a frightening time, not only for gay men, but for the public, as the exact cause was not well known. It was one of those things that was wrapped in so much fear that no one took the time to really understand and to know about the transmission and/or cause of the disease. Because I knew that Jeff was sick, I did my homework, and I learned that the disease could only be transmitted through body fluids and that people with AIDS were often shunned and discriminated against when they should be treated with kindness. The fear of AIDS was so intense that I was even refused health insurance because of my zip code, which was the Montrose area of Houston, where many gay men lived. Talk about discrimination! I was a heterosexual divorced mother of two and I could not get health insurance because of where I lived? After our lunch, Jeff and I started spending lots of time together. My daughters were with their dad every other weekend and I was teaching nursery school, so my school day was over by three p.m. if he needed some company. He would sometimes eat dinner with my daughters and me on week-ends, and he went with us to see *Sesame Street Live* at the Summit one Saturday in the spring. I will never forget that evening. When we got in my car, Jeff in the passenger seat, he pulled on his seat belt, only to start laughing hysterically. He could hardly talk he was laughing so hard, as there was a huge glob of bubble gum stuck on the seat belt. Not being a parent, I think it really surprised him and then made him laugh. Both of my daughters were in the back seat, but neither said a word. They acted like they had no idea where the gum came from, but I am sure that one of them was the culprit. Anyway, once Jeff got over the gum we headed on to *Sesame Street Live*. There were lots of yuppie parents in attendance with their children. We did not see anyone we knew, but we looked like we were the parents of these two little girls, and I think that Jeff enjoyed looking like he was a dad. He was really sweet with my daughters.

I'm not sure who had the most fun that evening, the parents or the children. The Count sang "Count" to the music of "Shout," a song made popular by the Isley Brothers, and I am sure that most of the adults who were dancing in the aisles that evening had danced to this song while in college. Jeff and I had a great time dancing and remembering a great band that played this song and many more great tunes at a frat party that we attended together while at UT. Such fond memories! This was a really good evening for all of us, with many laughs and positive energy.

There was another party that was fun, but rather tense, as the other guests were really giving Jeff the once-over. I was invited to a get-to-gether at a friend's home and I asked Jeff to go with me. This was shortly after our lunch, and I thought that it would be good to go to a party with our old friends, so we did. Jeff did not look good that evening. I found that with his diagnosis I could never be sure how he would feel or look. This particular evening, he had a sore that had suddenly appeared on his face that he tried to cover up, unsuccessfully, and he looked pale and drawn. We had a nice time, but since he was low on energy, we left early. My phone started ringing first thing the next morning with calls from friends who were yelling at me for exposing them to AIDS. They were sure that Jeff was infected even though I would not answer their questions about his health. I had learned by this time in my life that other people's business is not mine to tell, and I knew that Jeff would not want people to know. He had asked me after our lunch not to discuss his health with others or to tell any of our hometown friends, so I did not.

I became his support system. We talked about the 12 steps of AA and the emotional healing that people would experience. Jeff decided that he wanted to work the 12 steps with me as his guide, but not attend meetings unless they were with others who were in his condition. Louise Hay, a motivational speaker, was just becoming popular. She had a large following of gay men diagnosed with AIDS in the Los Angeles area. She held meetings that became known as The Hayride. She was one of the first to talk about healing your emotions in order to heal your body. She taught some techniques for healing that Jeff and I practiced together. I remember watching a video that she made, which was a new phenomenon in early 1988. It was a homemade video. Louise was sitting in front of a window, which was open, as the sheer curtains were gently swaying behind her and you could see traffic moving in the street beyond the window. Louise spoke in a soft, sweet, compassionate but determined voice. She gave instructions but was firm in her request. I remember that one of the exercises was to stand in front of a mirror and tell yourself, "I love you." I was surprised at how difficult that was for me to do, and then the instructions were to do this in front of a friend. I realize this sounds simple, but back in 1988, it was a huge step, as people were not as open with expressing their feelings. We discussed this process for a long time before we did it. It brought us closer to talk about how hard it was to even do it alone, but we were not sure we could do it in front of one another. After this long discussion, we decided to gut it up and do it; after all, it was only the two of us. Once we overcame our inhibitions and did it for the first time, it became easy, even in front of one another.

Jeff was impressed at how I had changed my life to a life of sobriety, and how I handled being a divorced mother of two little girls. He had known me as the loud party girl, and I had become the quiet and intro-spective spiritual seeker. We had always been close and honest with one another, but this was a whole new level of exposure for both of us. We kept our focus on healing and explored all of the different possibilities in Houston. Jeff wanted to start a support group based on the 12 steps. I knew that he had to start it. I could help, but in order for it to be suc-cessful, he would need to be the instigator. Meanwhile, he was working the steps himself. We spent a long time discussing the fourth step, which is a big one in 12-step communities. This step is where you really look at yourself and your life, at your shortcomings and your assets, and you write them down. There is usually lots of resistance to doing this step, but it is very healing. I will not say that it is pleasant because to admit to some of these things and then to really look at your behavior can bring up a lot of shame and self-loathing, but that is exactly the point. Once the fourth step is complete, it is good to move on to the fifth, which again can be scary, as you have to share your positives and negatives with another person. Jeff wanted healing and he wanted to be "right" with others, at least in his heart and mind.

Besides sharing with me, working the 12 steps, and studying

the lessons of Louise Hay, he found a place in California called the Simonton Cancer Center that offered retreats for patients with cancer, and most of the immune-system issues with AIDS were cancer. The first of its kind in the world, the center's integrated program was pioneered by cancer radiation oncologist, O. Carl Simonton, MD, who is often considered the "father of mind-body medicine" and author of the book *Getting Well Again*. Based in the field of psychoneuroimmunology, the Simonton method focuses on interactions between the mind and the body—how beliefs, attitudes, lifestyle choices, and spiritual and psychological perspectives impact our physiology and immune function, and how they can dramatically affect health, the course of disease, and our overall wellbeing.

Jeff wanted the two of us to attend one of these retreats, but it was too expensive. However, the director of the educational part of the program lived in Dallas and was in Dallas one week per month. After speaking with the staff at the center and determining that traveling to California was not possible, we made plans to go to Dallas for a long weekend to spend time with the educator of the center. We were both looking forward to learning more about the center and its philosophy, but just before we were to leave, Jeff ended up back in the hospital. He insisted that I go on ahead, so that at least one of us knew how to proceed with the program. I found the program very interesting and learned some things that I thought might help Jeff. Living a life of balance is very important, and I made a poster as a reminder of what needed to stay in focus. Unfortunately, even though Jeff was out of the hospital, he was no longer himself. He had lost ground and did not seem to be able to regain it, so implementing what I had learned in order to help him was futile, but what I learned in Dallas I am able to share with others facing a health challenge.

Jeff would call me to pick up his prescriptions for him, as I lived in the "gay" neighborhood with the pharmacies that carried the drugs used for HIV. I did not mind getting his prescriptions, but standing in line with others who were obviously ill with AIDS was my biggest challenge. Being empathic, it was difficult to look at the fear in their eyes and the sadness in their facial expressions. Many of them were wasting away; they were skin and bones from wasting disease, one of the results of AIDS. I knew that they were probably in this line because they were alone and did not have anyone to go to the pharmacy for them. Many gay men were abandoned by their partners when diagnosed, probably out of their own fear. The saddest part was that many young men were rejected by their family members because the family did not approve of their lifestyle; being gay was not acceptable. Guilt, shame, fear, and rejection were almost palpable in the Montrose area in the late eighties, as most of these young men were alone, isolated, and scared. They had no one to care for them when they could no longer care for themselves, and they often were out of money, as they had lost their jobs from suspicion and fear of their illness, or because they were not well enough to work. My friend Jeff was an exception in that his family was supportive; they did not turn their backs on him. However, they were uncertain of how to help and were not skilled at taking care of him, as he was beginning to waste away and looked very frail, like you might break his bones if you tried to pick him up when he could not walk.

In our quest for health and wellness, we began attending Christ Church Cathedral, an Episcopal church in downtown Houston, as we were fond of the dean of the cathedral and his messages. Many other gay men in the community began to attend here also, as there were messages of hope and the congregation was welcoming. The parishioners of this church realized the need for a place for these men who were alone to have a place to be taken care of and comforted in their process of dying, so the church established a place called the Omega House. I will never forget how nervous Jeff was when we went to meet with the female director of the facility to inquire what we might do to help. There was housing for three men, a "houseman," and volunteers who did their best to keep the patients comfortable. After Jeff got out of the hospital a second time, he went back to our hometown for a brief period, until the director called his parents and said there was a place for him. Even though his parents wanted to help him, I think that we all felt inadequate and knew that Omega House was the best place for him to be at this point in his illness. I was glad that he returned to Houston. The Omega House was not far from where I lived in Montrose, and at night after my daughters were asleep, I would inform the lady who lived with us that I was going to visit my friend, who she knew was very ill.

I felt like I was back in high school, sneaking out of the house, not for fun, but to spend time with my dear friend who was slipping away. It was interesting to me that all four of the men at Omega House during the time I was visiting were awake at night and asleep all day. I was never sure if it was because of their disease, their meds, or maybe that emotionally they did not like the darkness. After all, the lives they had been fighting to keep were surrounded in darkness due to their shame and guilt. I felt that Jeff had worked through most of the shame and guilt that he had, and even though we did not directly discuss his death, he seemed at peace.

By this time, it was November, with Thanksgiving just around the corner. I planned to take my girls to spend part of the holiday with my family in Bryan on Wednesday and Thursday nights. Then, on Friday morning I would meet their dad so that they could spend the rest of the holiday with him and I could go and sit with Jeff. We liked to watch *Dallas* together on Friday nights. I went by to see him on Wednesday morning before I left town to remind him that I would not be there for a couple of nights but that I would be back in time to watch *Dallas*. I went to remind him because his thinking was not as clear as it once had been. He had bad headaches, as his brain was beginning to be affected by his disease. My girls and I had a nice time visiting with relatives, but by Thursday night I was getting antsy. I was ready to leave to go back and spend time with Jeff, knowing that his parents were in Houston spending Thanksgiving with him. I still remember getting in the car to ride to my parents' home after visiting with cousins at my uncle's home out in the country. I had the strangest sensation; I felt lonely and anxious even though I was in the car with family and I was safe. When we got home I put my daughters to bed and went to sleep myself, only to get up very early the next morning before anyone else. I was in the kitchen making coffee when the phone rang and was answered by someone else in the house. It was only seven a.m. and I thought it was unusual that my parents would be getting a call so early in the morning. I was uncertain if they were even up. About fifteen minutes later, my stepmother, still in her robe, appeared in the kitchen. She had her back to me as she poured her coffee and told me that the call had been from one of her friends to tell her that Jeff Wilson had died on Thursday night. She did not see my face, but I was devastated. I was in shock because she had said it so matter-of-factly. I do not think I said a word. I had not told my parents about spending so much time with Jeff, as I was concerned that I would get "the lecture" and that they would not be supportive of me. I knew that they would be among those people who were still in fear from lack of knowledge. I felt it was better not to mention that I was the constant companion of Jeff. As I sat there in shock, I could not believe that he was gone, but realized that it must have happened during the time that I was in the car and felt so odd. She did say that he had passed away on Thursday night. I could not believe that I was not sitting by his side when he left, as I had imagined and planned in my head. It was hard to believe that he would not be there to watch *Dallas* that evening. How could he leave without my being there with him? How could I have not been there with him as he left? I felt angry at both of us and very, very sad. Jeff died Thursday night, Thanksgiving, November 24, 1988.

I was ready to leave, to get back to Houston as soon as possible, to find out exactly what had happened. How was he before he left his body? What happened after I left him on Wednesday? I drove my girls to meet their dad on my way back to Houston. We talked briefly about

Jeff's death and then I drove on to my home in Houston. This was before cell phones, but we did have answering machines. And mine was full of messages, some from Jeff asking me to come and sit with him, and several messages from the houseman who looked after him at Omega House. I felt really guilty that I wasn't there with him at the end. After listening to the messages and then sharing my sorrow and stories with my good friend and his law partner, I finally got myself over to Omega House to say goodbye to the space where I had last seen him and to talk with the houseman about what had happened. Once I felt like I had closure with everyone at Omega House, I drove over to Jeff's home in the Heights to visit with his parents. His parents were obviously sad but relieved that this nightmare was over. They were exhausted from watching their son fade away while there was absolutely nothing they could do. His mother explained to me that they had spent a good deal of time with him at Omega House on Thanksgiving but had decided to leave in the evening. He was not doing great and was asking for me, but they felt that they were okay to leave; that they would see him on Friday. Shortly after they had arrived at his house, the houseman called them and said that Jeff had taken a dramatic turn for the worse and that they should return immediately. He passed shortly before his parents walked back into his room.

The next big obstacle to be dealt with was the funeral home. None of the funeral homes that his parents would have chosen would deal with the corpses of the men who died of AIDS. It might hurt their business, and I assume that there were some of those still in fear. The funeral home that would take Jeff's body dealt with mostly indigent people, was in a rough part of town, and in a very creaky, musty old house that had creepy shadows playing on the walls, but the caretaker was very compassionate and thoughtful. He realized that he had a booming business because of the refusal of other funeral directors, but he appeared to be determined to help the families who lost their loved one to AIDS to feel as comfortable as possible, even though they were out of their element.

Jeff's service was held at the chapel of Christ Church Cathedral, and there were a number of friends there from our hometown. Several of the females came up to me after the service and asked me why I did not tell them that Jeff was sick. They were actually angry with me, and I assume that they were informed that Jeff and I had spent many hours together. I just looked at them and responded that it was not my place to tell them. If Jeff had wanted them to know, he would have told them himself.

I cherish the time I was able to spend with Jeff and grateful to learn more about him, myself, and the death process. He enlightened me about alternative lifestyles and introduced me to others who are like me except for their sexual preference in a partner. These people termed "gay" love just as deeply as any heterosexual. I was thankful to have some skills to help him to heal himself and to come to a place of peace. I missed him terribly and had to work to forgive myself for not being with him when he passed.

Discovering the Power
of My Mind

In 1990, I was living in Houston with my two daughters: one in preschool, one in second grade. In the fall, my girls' dad told me that he was not going to be able to continue to give me the same child support. His job was changing, and he wasn't going to be making as much money anymore. As a matter of fact, he didn't know if he would even be able to keep his job. So I needed to be thinking about what I was going to do, because I relied on the child support for my house payment. I was not making a lot teaching nursery school, a job I took in order to spend more time with my girls. Another benefit was that my younger daughter had free tuition to St. Luke's Methodist Church's children's program. It was a good program for her and for me as a teacher. This was where we went to church, and I enjoyed working with all the teachers. The director was fantastic. She was always looking out for those of us who worked for her.

In late fall, I was beginning to get a little anxious, thinking about the cost of living in Houston and how working and raising my two daughters by myself didn't allow me a lot of free time. I didn't get to spend much time with my friends, so why was I living here? It was expensive to live in Houston, and I lived in a specific area of Houston to make me feel like I lived in a small town. So maybe I should just move to a small town. Hmm, where could I go? Well, I had grown up in a small town. My parents and sister still lived there, while my brother lived in the sister city. Maybe I should think about returning, even though when I left in 1968 I swore I'd never return.

When I began considering this move I did not say anything to my family, but I decided that I would apply to teach at the two different school districts: one in Bryan and the other in the sister city of College Station. Maybe there would be some openings in January and I would be able to get a job and start at midterm. I got applications from both school districts and filled them out. I grew up in Bryan, where my father was on the school board the entire time I was in school, and my sister had been teaching for Bryan ISD for many years. I did not have any connections in the administration office in either town, so I just sent in my applications, sat back, and waited.

I did talk to the director of the nursery school about my financial stress, and I wanted her to be on alert that I might need to find something else so that I could afford to take care of my girls. The girls were with their dad at Christmas for about a week, and while they were gone I did a lot of reading. I read one book in particular called *The Superbeings: Overcoming Limitations Through the Power of the Mind,* by John Randolph Price. John Randolph Price was a new thought author and teacher. He was writing books about manifesting and the law of attraction many years before *The Secret* or some of the other law of attraction materials became known to a wider range of the public.

Superbeings made me feel great. It helped me to stay in a positive state of mind and not get into "woe is me" or the anxiety of "what's going to happen?" Just knowing that I would be taken care of brought me peace. I had been studying with a teacher named Pat who had gone to Unity Ministerial School. She was an excellent teacher and had taught me many things, including the laws of manifestation, but it was nice to read a book that incorporated the things that I had learned from her with a little bit of a different slant. In the book, John Randolph Price describes how we have the capacity within us to draw to us what we want and need, and he suggested being specific, making a list and describing in detail exactly what you want or need. An example would be: a white silk blouse with long billowy sleeves, a pointed collar, buttons up the front in a size 8 from Saks, instead of simply a white blouse. So I started thinking about what specifically I wanted, a very nice daydream for me to keep myself entertained while my girls were away.

I decided that I would write about each area of my life starting with my career. If I had the perfect job, what would it be? Hmm. Well, I really enjoyed teaching. I loved kids and I liked watching them learn, seeing what excited them, and how I could help them to attain information. I enjoyed working with their parents. I had taught students who are dyslexic and I really enjoyed trying to figure out what little key might open their mind to be able to understand something, to absorb it and to grasp it. I also liked working with their parents and helping them to understand their children and how to be an advocate for them.

Besides being a teacher, I had my certification as a chemical dependency counselor, and I had done some counseling, not only with adults, but also with children whose parents were in 12-step programs. I really enjoyed working with these kids and helping them to understand their feelings and what was going on in their homes and how they could have better relationships with their siblings and their parents. After listing what I enjoyed, I realized that I was describing the job of a drug education coordinator for a school district. I put a name to it and listed all the things I wanted to do while working in this capacity.

I would be able to work with adults to teach parenting classes, with teachers to help them with drug education lessons for their classrooms, and to do some presentations myself with the kids, so that I would be able to work with children and also do some counseling if needed. I wrote more specific details for each of these areas and then moved on to my living situation, writing about "the perfect house."

The house I lived in I loved, but it was an older house built in the twenties and it was near the freeway, so it was noisy and needed more updating than I had the time or money for. So there were some things that I would change in a new living situation to make my life easier. I sat and thought about what would be the perfect house. This is what I came up with: It would have two living spaces—one, a living room, and then a large family room; the adjoining kitchen would have an island for food prep and a breakfast area. I wanted to have four bedrooms: one for each daughter, a guestroom and a master. I longed for a nice-sized closet for myself and a garden-like bathroom where light came in with a Jacuzzi bathtub and a separate shower. I wanted ceiling fans in every room, an automatic garage door opener with the garage attached to the house so I wouldn't have to get wet when I was carrying groceries in from the car. I also needed to have the laundry area in the house, and I wanted a sprinkler system so I didn't have to water the yard with hoses and sprinklers myself. I wished for high ceilings in the family room, with a fireplace. I wanted a powder room and a bathroom for my daughters with a sink for each of them.

After writing my wish list, I looked it over to make adjustments. I felt all warm inside. Absorbing the feeling of receiving the perfect job and living in the perfect house felt like Christmas morning as a little girl. One thing that I did not specify was the location of the job or the house. I was open to wherever I was led. I smiled to myself and even though I had worked with this exercise before on a smaller scale, this time felt different, like I finally really "got it" on a cellular level. I blessed each list, and then I put them away in my dresser drawer. Every now and then I would think about those lists and get that warm, fuzzy feeling all over again. *Hmm, it would really be nice if I had those things, and my life would be easier,* I'd think, but I didn't dwell on it. I didn't long for it. I just remembered that I had written those things down, which helped me to stay in a positive state of mind instead of going into the gutter worrying about what might happen if I couldn't come up with the money for the mortgage. I was anticipating the arrival of my "lists" with the excitement of Christmas surprises—what a wonderful feeling to recall!

December came and went with no information from either of the school districts, no inquiries, no jobs. I continued to teach nursery school and to wonder what was next. The preschool director knew that I was looking for other employment and going on interviews to teach in Houston ISD, but I still had not found another job. I didn't know what I was going to do, but I knew that I was going to need to do something soon.

Around the second week in January, I took my girls out to dinner and when we returned home, the girl who was living with us in return for childcare told me that a man from College Station ISD by the name of Dr. Burnett had called at about seven-thirty that night. He had asked to speak to me and said that he would call back the next evening, which he did. I answered the phone, he introduced himself, and told me he had gone over to the human resources department of the school administration and was looking over job applications. While going through them, he saw that I had my chemical dependency license and he was looking for a drug education coordinator. I almost fell off the bed that I was sitting on. He began to read the list of duties that I would have: working with parents, working with students and teachers, and providing parenting classes and possibly some counseling. I was checking off in my mind the list of things that I had written on that piece of paper after reading *Superbeings*. I was stunned. He was describing exactly what I had written as my perfect job! I hate to admit this, but I had a hard time believing that he was going down my entire list. And then doubt would be replaced with joy and giggly excitement! He asked if I could come for an interview. I replied that I could be in College Station on Friday to meet with him. This was Tuesday, so I made plans to go visit my parents for the weekend and have this job interview. I arrived on Friday, early in the afternoon, for the group interview. I was interviewed not only by Dr. Burnett, who had set up the interview, but also by a group of counselors who led the drug education programs in their schools and a couple of other administrators. They asked me questions.

I answered them. I felt like the interview went really well, and then it was over. I fully expected them to offer me the job on the spot, but that didn't happen. I knew that this was my job, the one that I had written about back in December. I had pulled out my list from the drawer to make sure that Dr. Burnett had correctly described my job, and he had! What I did not know at the time of the interview is that the job had to be posted for a certain number of days before being filled.

I spent the rest of the weekend with my parents, who by now were getting excited about the possibility of grandchildren being near them. I was just wondering what was going to happen next. I went back to Houston on Sunday and to work on Monday. The director of the day school asked me about my appointment. I told her it went really well, so she was beginning to get a little anxious about finding a replacement for me, but I didn't know for sure if I had the job because they had not offered it to me. She asked if I would call at the end of the week if I still had not heard from the school district. The end of the week came and no word, so I called Dr. Burnett. He told me that I had been approved, but that the offer had to come from the director of Human Resources. He thought that he was going to call me, but he just didn't know when.

Another week went by and finally on Friday morning, I got a telephone call before leaving to go teach school from the Human Resource director at College Station ISD, who offered me the job as the drug education coordinator and asked me if I could start in two weeks. "Sure, I can start in two weeks," I replied.

Now, remember, I had two small children, two dogs, a house full of stuff and no place to live. But, sure, I could start in two weeks. We hung up the phone. I was so excited. I was going to Bryan the next day, Saturday, for a funeral for one of my family's dear friends. I drove into Bryan, went straight to the funeral, and after it was over, I called my sister-in-law who lived in College Station and asked if she could recommend a College Station real estate broker; she could—her neighbor.

She gave me the info and I called the Realtor to set up an appointment to look at some property on Sunday, the next day.

I'd been struggling financially, not able to make ends meet. I was living on credit cards. So I told this Realtor that I needed something that was assumable or a house that I could rent. She said, "There is nothing. There is nothing." This was a time when the university did not have enough housing. Students were having to live in other small towns around Bryan College Station and commute to school. I did have a neighbor in Houston whose father had been a professor and his parents had recently moved out of their home, so there was a possibility that I would be able to rent that house if I couldn't find something else. But they weren't sure that I would be able to do it in two weeks.

As the Realtor was telling me there was nothing available, in my mind I kept saying to myself, *I forgive you because I know that's not true.* We made an agreement to meet the next day. My stepmother and I looked at a "For Sale by Owner" before meeting with the Realtor. The Realtor showed us a couple of properties, but none were really that appealing. The Realtor told me later that she could look at my stepmother and know that she was thinking, *My granddaughters are not going to live here.* So after we had looked at all the available properties the Realtor had been able to line up, she said, "Well, there are some new houses a few streets over. Would you like to look at those?"

We went over to a new area of town. A new subdivision was being built on the prairie, and there were several recently completed houses on the street. I didn't know how I could afford new housing, but hey, I decided to look anyway. The Realtor opened the front door to the first house we were going to look at, a house that had just been completed. It was move-in ready. I walked in and there was a living room to the right. Behind the living room was a large family room with a vaulted ceiling and a fireplace. On the other side of that was the kitchen with an island and a breakfast area, and a washer and dryer inside the house behind louvered doors. We walked down the hallway where there was a powder room. There were two bedrooms in the front of the house and a bathroom with two sinks, then a third bedroom and the master. The master had a nice-sized closet, a Jacuzzi bathtub, and a separate shower like I requested. It had glass bricks along the wall, so there was lots of light coming in. There was a ceiling fan in every room and a garage that adjoined the house with a garage door opener, and there was a sprinkler system. Again, everything I had written on the piece of paper describing the perfect house. I was overwhelmed. It is difficult to describe how I felt.

The feeling in my body was unbelievable. I knew it was my house the minute I walked in, even before I saw the many things that I had written on the piece of paper. I knew it was my house just like I had known that it was my job! It was exactly what I had written and what I had envisioned. Unfortunately, I needed to leave, as I was out of time. I needed to go meet the girls, who were with their dad and were to be picked up on my way back to Houston. I had to take my stepmother home and on the way I asked her if she thought my dad might possibly loan me the money for the down payment until I could sell my house in Houston. She said she didn't know, but she was thinking the same thing and would go home and ask him.

I drove back to Houston on cloud nine, and as my teacher, Pat, would say, "It's like a hot knife through butter." Everything seemed to line up perfectly, and it did. I got the house. I got the job. We moved in two weeks. It was perfect. Even though it all happened many years ago, I still am amazed at how perfectly everything worked out. I stayed in a positive state of mind. Every time I started to get anxious, I would think about my list and about how wonderful it was going to be when all those things came to pass. Believe me, it was wonderful when it came to pass, as I had a great job and a great house. I'm very grateful that my list of requests came to fruition just as John Randolph Price had described. The key to successful manifestation is the elevated emotion of joy supported by expectation.

Not Gonna Just Stand There
and Look Pretty Anymore

I am a very lucky lady. I come from a family of landowners, farmers, and ranchers who have been kind enough to leave some of their property to me. My father passed away in 2008, and I inherited, along with my daughters, a piece of farmland that was not only good for crop production, but it also had an oil well on it. While the well is on our property, the oil in the ground is owned by my three siblings and me. Just having an oil well on your property does not make you rich, as wells produce less and less over the years, but to maintain the lease, oil companies are required to produce a minimum amount of oil.

The lease for this well was signed in 1989, had been sold a couple of times, and was not a very favorable lease for my family. It was probably a great lease for the 1980s, but not for 2013. Any decision that I made about oil and gas production on my property would also affect my siblings. I would have to deal with the oil company and have the pad on my property, but any oil and gas accumulated and paid for would be divided among my siblings and me.

Around November 15, 2013, I received a letter from the oil company that held the lease titled a "RELEASE OF ALL CLAIMS". I read the letter, which in my opinion had a very hostile tone and felt like a warning from Big Oil. The tone came across as: "We're coming to violate your property and you can't do anything about it. We might pay you a little bit, but we're going to have our way with you." I was so stunned and angry that the letter was shaking in my hand! After a time, my anger began to subside and my physical symptoms of anger calmed down. I felt my pounding heart slowing down, the redness in my cheeks cooling, and my trembling hand becoming steady. Oh, but those thoughts of Big Oil and the little guy. I very much felt like the little guy, but even worse, I was a female dealing with a very masculine profession, run by good ole boys, that were, in my opinion, smooth talkers who were very impressed with themselves, especially if they had "made it" and had lots of money. This letter reminded me that oil companies basically can do whatever they want, especially in Texas! This reality would really settle in over the next few months.

I did not know what to do, and not wanting to be reactive, I did nothing. The following day, I got a telephone call from the surface land man who had sent me the "RELEASE OF ALL CLAIMS" document, explaining that he had mistakenly sent me the wrong papers, and that he should have sent a Surface Use Agreement. But the damage was done, and we were off to a bad start as far as I was concerned.

I was asked to please disregard the papers that I had received the previous day and that I should receive the correct papers in a day or so. He also wanted me to meet him out on my property to discuss where to place their new pad to drill the wells they planned to drill. We made arrangements to meet the next afternoon. I drove out to the property, which is located in The Bottom—the Brazos River Bottom—to meet this fellow, Paul, who was employed by the oil company. I realized as soon as I arrived that he had already met with the relatives who rent my property to grow their crops, as they did when my father, a partner in ownership, was alive. We had a "lease" that could have been written on a cocktail napkin. It was written by the tenants who set the terms of the lease and set the price, something that also began while my father was alive. It was a "relative" type of agreement, which I was okay with, as they were looking after my property and they knew the property because they had been working it for years.

The land man and my uncle had previously discussed the best possible location of the drill pad in relation to the existing oil well pad and farming practices. We walked around while the land man shared information about the best location for the pad for the oil company and for my tenants, and then we talked about what they intended to do. They planned to drill four horizontal wells going southeast one way, and if they were good wells, which they thought they would be, then they might want to come back and drill several more going the opposite direction. Lots of wells meant lots of money. Was I not excited? No.

I know that most people think, "Oh, an oil well is wonderful," but that's not me. Yes, money is nice, but I was thinking about the damage to the property, all the pollution, and I knew these would be frack wells because they were horizontal and that type of well involves fracking, using tons of water with added chemicals in order to get the oil and gas out of the ground. I guess I am more of an environmentalist than a capitalist.

While we were discussing placement of the pad, I brought up the issue of fracking with the land man, who I caught shooting a quick glance at my uncle before each of them rolled their eyes. I could hear them thinking, *Oh yeah, she's one of those. I told you about her. She's one of those tree huggers, a stupid environmentalist.* But I continued to ask questions. How much water would they use, what did they do with it after fracking, did they leave it in the ground where they were fracking or did they remove it and, if so, where did they take it? And the most important question: Where were they going to get the water for the fracking?

The surface land man said to me, "We are going to pump the water from the river." Remember, I said this was in the Brazos River Bottom, so the Brazos River was not far away, but there were several landowners between my property and the river, so I knew that they would have to get an easement from each property owner in order to lay the pipe to pump the water to my property.

I asked him if they had started getting the easements, and he said, "No, that is not in my department." Someone else would be doing that, and if they did not get the water from the river, they would use some of Mr. Tanner's water, referring to my relative and tenant.

My head snapped around fast as I turned and looked him right in the eye and said, "It is *not* Mr. Tanner's water. It is *my* water."

He didn't say anything, but he was locked in a stare with me, and he knew that I meant what I said.

I received the correct papers from him a couple days later. I was concerned about the fracking water, to be sure; and I was also concerned about fracking, period!

All oil companies seem to repeatedly do this. They come in and they want it done last week, so they put lots of pressure on you to hurry up and get the papers signed because, "The rig is coming, the rig is coming, the rig will be here soon to drill. We are on the schedule and we cannot miss our turn. We've got to hurry. We've got to get this done and that done." They are the ones who make the schedules, not me. Anyway, again, I felt pushed. I felt like I was being pressured to hurry and make a decision, and frankly, I did not like it. There was really no decision, as they could basically do what they wanted because they held the lease. They just needed my signature, but looking back over this entire incident, I did not know why they even needed my signature. They did what they wanted, disregarding the legal documents that the oil company's legal counsel signed.

In the course of passing papers back and forth between my attorney and the attorney for the oil company, I voiced my concerns about the water under my property, my water, with my attorney, so he suggested, "Let's just put it in this Surface Use Agreement that they cannot use your water without your permission."

"Great! What a wonderful idea. Why didn't I think of that?" I was feeling so much like the victim that I was not thinking clearly.

The next time the documents came our way for review, we added a paragraph that the oil company could not use the water under my property without my written permission. A cover letter went with that revision to the oil company's attorneys for their review, along with a copy for the land man. The provision was there stating that they could not use my water without written permission from me, and the representative from the oil company signed the document. This document was given to the surface land man who I had met with so that he saw it, I signed it, and the representative from the oil company signed it. I felt protected because the papers said if they were going to use my water, then they would have to ask me. We would discuss it.

Water at that time for fracking was going for 25 to 50 cents a barrel, a barrel of water being 31.5 to 31 gallons. I did my homework. I was still hoping and thinking that they were going to get the water from the river as Paul had stated. A couple of months went by, and the oil company came in and put the pad down. The rig arrived and they began to drill. I went out to the site one day to watch them using all their computers for doing the drilling and putting the pipe down in the hole. It was very interesting to watch in real time on the computer screen. My, how things have changed!

I went a few weeks later to check on the progress. The rig was gone and there were several trailers around the pad site. I knocked on the door of the trailer that appeared to be the office. A man opened the door and allowed me in. I told him and the other man that I was the owner of the property and I was there to see how the production was coming along. They did not ask if I wanted to sit down, if I wanted a cup of coffee, nothing. I asked again how things were going. They said everything was going smoothly. They assured me that I didn't need to worry about anything (I've heard that before) and I could just go home and collect my check. It was a very condescending statement. I thought that they were rude. I was irritated once again by men treating me like I was stupid and that money was the most important thing in the world, more important than what we are doing to the earth and the air and … what about the water?

During this time, my daughters' father was very ill. His illness began progressing swiftly, and he passed away on March 31, 2014. I was doing my best to stay in Houston to be available to our daughters, to comfort them and to help them walk through losing their dad. I was glad that I could be with them, to be supportive.

A couple months after my daughters' dad's death, I decided I needed a break. I needed to go someplace to get filled up because I was an empty vessel. I noticed that Deepak Chopra and Jean Houston were having an event in Sedona, Arizona, a great place with wonderful energy, and these are both fabulous teachers. I signed up.

I went to this event, met some interesting people, heard some intriguing talks, learned some enlightening lessons, and I returned home feeling revitalized. It was a fabulous experience, well worth the time and money. Shortly after I returned home, I spoke with my sister, who told me that there were lots of water trucks on my property and I should go out and take a look. So, the next day, my friend and I drove out to the site in my car. She had on new flip-flops and I had on new tennis shoes, which became important a little later. My friend Rose was driving. I suggested that we drive down what's called a turn row because the main road into the area was busy and congested with large trucks going in and out. A turn row is a dirt road that is used to drive farm vehicles on. It is compacted dirt, not paved but hard. A tractor can turn around on a turn row and head back down the field in the opposite direction. We were driving down this turn row when I saw water coming out of the backs of some of these water trucks. There were probably sixty or seventy yellow trucks that they had filled with water in order to frack with high pressure. I saw the water leaking, and I saw that the road was beginning to look darker in color ahead of us, probably due to the road being wet. I suggested that we stop and turn around. We should not continue to drive forward because we might get stuck.

Rose replied, "Oh no. Not a problem. We won't get stuck."

A couple more feet, and the tires began to spin; we were stuck. We could not make it to the water trucks, so we could not see the pad or really anything that was happening. We could just see all these water trucks. We couldn't go forward, and we couldn't go backwards, and neither one of us wanted to get out and step in the muddy red dirt. Besides that, what could we do, anyway? We were two weak women. We couldn't push this car out of the mud. I called my tenants and asked for some assistance in getting unstuck.

My cousin and one of his sons, who was about to graduate from high school, came to try and pull us out. They attached a chain from my back bumper to his truck and they pulled and they pulled. Nothing happened. Everybody's wheels were spinning. A few minutes later, it stopped. I felt my cousin unhook the chain from his truck, and he backed away from my car. His son got out of the truck and came over to my side of the car and said his dad was going to get the four-wheel-drive truck because they hadn't been able to pull us out with just the regular truck.

He was in his boots, and he walked around to where they were working on the oil pad, so he was out of sight. A few minutes later, he came walking back to the car and we chatted about his graduation and the practice he attended in the morning and what all he was going to be doing during the summer. I asked him how they got the water from the river to fill all of these trucks and he answered, "Oh, no. They didn't get the water from the river. We drilled two new water wells." I let that soak in, and I could feel my blood pressure rising. I did not say a word, to him, to my friend, to anyone. If I had opened my mouth, I probably would have screamed. I was furious.

I kept my mouth closed. I'm sure steam was coming out of my ears. My cousin returned with the four-wheel-drive truck and we got unstuck, turned around, and went home. As soon as I got home and my friend left, I called my attorney to confirm that drilling those two water wells was illegal if what I was told could possibly be correct. He was shocked that something like this had happened and that I had no idea about it and yes, it would be illegal.

Again, I wasn't sure what to do. I felt like I had been betrayed and very much taken advantage of, not only by the oil company but by my relatives, who had cooperated. I had originally questioned the oil company about a depth clause in the original lease, and they had basically pooh-poohed me, telling me that they were in the right and that, no, they didn't have to listen to me questioning them about this depth clause.

At this point, I decided that I wanted to call someone who lived elsewhere—not in Brazos County where I lived, not in a surrounding county, but away from here. I called a friend of mine who I had dated some after college, who was an oil and gas attorney in Houston. I told him what had happened, and he was very interested in the depth clause. To him, the water was minor since that was not his field of expertise. He did allow that someday there would probably be a showdown at the Texas State Capitol between Big Oil and water rights. He was willing to pursue dealing with the oil company, using the water issue as leverage.

If the depth clause was indeed correct, there was a possibility that we could get our percentage of royalty changed and the original lease renegotiated, which would benefit not only myself but my siblings as well. I sent my attorney a copy of all the papers that I had. He wrote a letter to the oil company. As expected, they have in-house attorneys and don't have to pay extra for any of their legal work, and basically their attorney pooh-poohed my attorney's offer to forgive them if they would change our percentage, forgive them for not honoring the depth, and for stealing my water. He did not say it that way, but he used his legalese to make those points.

Basically, the response to his letter was, "So what?" My attorney and

I were trying to decide what to do. In the meantime, my daughter, who attended law school and is interested in water law, started investigating and asked for copies of the water permits. One of her friends, who had begun working for my friend, Robert, requested copies of the water permits from the water district that governs our property. Upon receipt, we learned that of my historic use permits, which were permits that were granted by the water district as to how much water had been used in the past for my property, four had been reduced to equal the exact amount of water the oil company said they had used to frack the wells on my property. Hmm, an interesting development that I did not like!

Once again I felt angry and betrayed, as my cousin, who was a partner in the group that rented my property, was on the water board. Interesting how my historic use permits were reduced without my knowledge, or permission, to the exact amount that the oil company needed. Things were beginning to get even fishier.

In the process of requesting copies of the water permits, we got copies of papers that identified my relative as the owner of my property and my water. It was signed by him and notarized by the surface land man. Remember Paul? He was the one who I told that the water was my water. I was livid. It was very hard for me to believe that I had been betrayed by this relative, Don, who I had known all my life, and also by a young man who I deliberately told the water was my water. It was not like he didn't know, and on top of that, the oil company had agreed to the terms that I had placed in the Surface Use Agreement by signing the document! What good were those legal contracts?

I felt, once again, betrayed by men and taken advantage of, and very angry at my experience with betrayal and men, and the dishonesty, the blatant lying and stealing, and acting like it was fine because I was just being a hysterical woman. I don't know if the moral compass was not there, but obviously money was more important to them than values or family. Remember when I said I should be excited that I have an oil well? Something in me is different. I'm more concerned about the land

and about integrity, and I am very disappointed when I find out that greed, greed, greed supersedes all moral values these days.

What really burned me was that all of the people involved claimed to be Christian. Even the land man was talking about going to Baylor, that Baptist University in Waco. What do they teach? What hypocrites! I would like to call the land man's mother!

To me, this behavior was sad and caused so much pain and suffering. If people would just do the right thing and not sell themselves out for the almighty dollar, I believe our world would be a better place. My dealings with the oil company and with my attorney were all kind of hit-and-miss for a while. My attorney still wanted to pursue a lawsuit against the oil company. I wasn't certain. I wasn't sure how much it was going to cost me, and then all of a sudden, the oil company came back at the end of 2014 and they wanted to put in another pad in order to drill more wells with the pipe going in the opposite direction.

Again, it was, "Hurry up, hurry up, hurry up." I called my attorney. He said not to sign anything until he could review the papers. A couple of days later, I got an email from him that he was having a major medical procedure, and then a couple of days after that, I got an email saying he had a triple bypass and he would be away from work for a while, and that my issue had been turned over to one of his partners.

I was distraught because now I felt like I had to start all over explaining the whole situation to a new person who I didn't know. Again, "Hurry up, hurry up, hurry up." The surface use papers were given to me again, but this time, the oil company agreed to pay me for the water that they had stolen in the past minus the cost of the water wells that I did not authorize. They wanted to pay me a mere ten cents a barrel, which was the price that my uncle and my cousin had agreed to previously.

Don kept telling me that he wasn't getting paid; he said he was just getting a pivot, you know, one of those watering systems that waters from the top while slowly moving in a circle. If you are getting a pivot, that costs money, and I was getting tired of the runaround from him and his refusal to answer my questions directly. During about my sixth conversation with him, trying to get things straight, trying to get him to apologize and do the right thing, to pay me, he finally admitted he was getting ten cents a barrel. I told him that was a bad deal, but he had done it because that was what somebody else had done. Again, greed outweighed logic, which led to him making a poor decision. If you are going to be greedy, be really greedy, and do not give the water away!

The thing I hated most about the entire situation, after I got over the betrayal, was that now I needed to do something. I had been taken advantage of several times by men and I realized that each time it was a little worse. I needed to stop this pattern now. I could not really let this one go because I could not imagine what would happen next if I did not stand up for myself. I hated continuing to ask for remediation, with nothing happening. I was tired of being ignored. I'm sure my relatives thought that I would give up and go away. But I felt that the only option left was to file a lawsuit to protect my rights.

I pondered this dilemma for weeks, and one day, after a phone conversation with my new water attorney, I looked up above my computer to see the picture that I have hanging on my wall for inspiration. It is a picture of my great-grandmother, Ida Van Zandt Jarvis. This photo portrays her as an older woman, slight in stature, but from the stories I have heard about her, her size does not match up with her determination and progressive actions. Ida and her husband, J.J. Jarvis, were very involved with the Christian church and assisted in the return of AddRan, a male and female Christian college in Fort Worth, Texas, where it had been located prior to moving to Thorpe Springs and Waco. The name was changed to Texas Christian University, TCU. Ida was the first female trustee of TCU; she donated money to the university; and the first female dorm there bears the name Jarvis Hall. Ida persuaded her husband, a Major in the Confederacy, to donate land that they owned in East Texas to establish a college for African Americans, which was first known as the Jarvis Christian Institute and later became Jarvis Christian College; it is still in operation in Hawkins, Texas. Not only was Ida instrumental in the establishment of the school, she realized that having only an education would not serve the students well; that they would be more widely accepted if they were also exposed to social graces. Ida had a faculty member choose five students every month to be put on the train to Fort Worth to stay in the Jarvis home for a week and learn etiquette and proper manners. She was truly a woman before her time! I am certain that this monthly event must have been a hard sell for Ida, but she knew it was the correct thing to do and she did it! I knew the right thing to do even though I was reluctant to do it—namely, file a lawsuit.

I would be "ruffling feathers," as I am sure Ida did, and I knew that most females in the family would just be quiet, but that did not feel right. Sometimes you have to stand up for your beliefs even if they are unpopular. I can hear the comments from other family members: "This is family—you do not do this to family." Oh, really? What was done to me by family?

Besides my own torment, I also thought of the collective of women who have not been able to stand up for themselves, who have not been able to find their voice. I needed to change the paradigm for women in my family and in Texas. I knew that I would be blamed somehow. Even though I was the one whose property was damaged and stolen, I would end up being the bad guy, especially with my family. I spoke with my daughters about this, and I told them what would probably happen, namely that their cousins might not have anything to do with them any longer. Both girls agreed that we needed to file suit against our relatives even though we did not want to do it. It was not about the money; however, being repaid for all of the legal expenses would be great. I had to do something different, not only for me but for all women. An admission of wrongdoing, an apology, and payment for my water would have saved everyone anguish, money, legal fees, and probably embarrassment on their part, but since none of those things happened, I decided my only recourse was to file suit. I had made six phone calls and three in person visits, including one with my daughters and cousin present, and there was still denial and no action by my tenants. I guess they expected me to continue to "stand there and look pretty, darlin'."

I had my attorney move forward with sending a letter to them, letting them know what was about to happen. I even sent a letter letting Don know that he would be hearing from my attorney. I did not realize that he would receive this letter the weekend of his birthday when all of his children were in town. A few days later, an attorney with whom I had worked on some other family property matters called and told me that my relatives had asked him to represent them against me. He did not want to do it if I felt like it would be a conflict. I really liked this attorney and was pleased that he would ask me. I was delighted that he would represent them, as they needed him and I knew that he would be fair.

I finally had their attention; they learned to give it to me the hard way, after over a year of ignoring me. I guess they thought that I would remain the "nice girl" and be quiet. Wrong girl. I got the Universe's message that it was time to speak up for myself. This time, I needed to take direct action.

I had hoped to get even with the oil company, but since they had in-house counsel and I did not, it was costing me a lot of money to try to get them to admit wrongdoing, even though they offered to pay me for the water they had stolen. They needed water for the next fracking, and we talked about them using my water, but I was unwilling to sell it to them for the rock-bottom price of ten cents a barrel. So guess who they had worked out a deal with? My relatives. I think they already had the deal worked out before they made the offer to me because they could get such a good deal from them. They also provided water for another well across the road from our community property or my sister's property for a well drilled on a friend's land. At least, he was a friend until he got screwed out of his water deal.

The attorney who was hired to defend my relatives suggested that we have a chat. I had gone to them three times in person already, so it was time for them to come to me. We met at a local bakery/sandwich shop and I finally got an "I made a mistake" admission from Don, not a full-out apology but a statement of recognition that they had done me wrong. As part of our agreement, we were going to have an actual lease, not one that they presented to me, as they did when my dad was still living, but a lease with actual descriptions of what was allowed and what was not and the price of the lease each year, increasing regularly since that was an issue also. They had been getting the "relative" rate, but no more. At least, it was not going to be a rate they chose!

We had to negotiate the length of the lease. I was not in favor of a five-year term, as I was still not sure that I could trust them and was not convinced that I should even lease to them again, but the family issue won out. We came to an agreement on legal fees and a portion of the amount that I felt they owed me for the water. I did not feel completely satisfied, but the settlement was something that I could live with, cautiously.

Just as I predicted, I am now treated as the bad guy. I have limited interactions with my cousins. We do talk, but there is still some angst I feel from them. How could I do that to their dad? I do speak and work with my uncle, as we do still have business together. I have forgiven him and my cousin. Trust is still an issue, but hopefully that can be restored with time. I learned long ago that a grudge is too heavy to carry and a detriment to all; forgiveness is the key.

There were days when I had to really muster up my courage to move forward, as I felt forced to take action that I did not want to take, which is why it took me over three years to get this resolved. I had hoped I would receive an apology and that we could come to an agreement. Even though it was difficult to take legal action, I know that I did the right thing, not only for myself, but for all women.

I am happy and relieved to have found my voice, no more uncomfortable feelings of denying myself or playing small, this was a long, painful lesson, but I appreciate each of my teachers, and feel that I can check this Life Lesson as Learned! I can finally be my authentic self. I spoke up/stood up for myself and I am still standing. It is great to BE EMPOWERED!

Have you ever had to do the "right" thing, even if you did not want to do it?

Epilogue

I want to express gratitude for my teachers: the people in my life who presented me with challenging situations, to learn about myself, to look at what needed to be changed in me, and doing my best to change myself. Without these people, I would not have found my voice.

My wish in sharing these stories is to inspire others to stand up for themselves, to find their voice and permission to write their story, as everyone has a story from which we each can learn.

If you would like to receive a copy of the Ho'Oponopono prayer that I used in the opening story, you can get a free copy on line at: womenhealingtheworld.com or MarySueRabe.com

I hope you have enjoyed reading these stories and the lessons that I have learned.

About the Author

Mary Sue Rabe grew up in a small town in Central Texas in a conservative Southern environment. She was encouraged to go to college to get her "MRS" degree and find herself a good husband, but she was also encouraged to get a teaching certificate to have something to fall back on– just in case. After her marriage didn't work out, she became a single, working mother of two small daughters and took a job teaching children with learning disabilities.

There were few resources to help women in her position at that time. She struggled during those years financially, but she began exploring personal growth, metaphysics, energy healing, women's empowerment, mindset enhancement, and enjoyed the freedom of living life on her own terms.

Mary Sue enjoys the company of her furry friends, Sophie and Dakota, rescued Great Pyrenees, and her granddog, Mona, a rescued Pyr/Golden Retriever mix, as well as spending time by the river at her home in Wimberley, Texas, hosting retreats for women.

Now in her retirement years, with decades of experience in teaching, training, mentoring, counseling, bio field healing and providing/promoting events to expand consciousness, Mary is excited to have birthed Women Healing the World. Together with other women in her state of Texas and others around the country and the world, they are bringing the feminine power of healing to those in need, to make a better world for everyone.

Further Resources

If you'd like to book Mary Sue Rabe for a speaking engagement, interview, or mentoring go to Contact us: https://womenhealingtheworld.com/contact

To learn more about Women Healing the World go here:

https://womenhealingtheworld.com

or

MarySueRabe.com 979 255 8281